Thanksgiving Day ha: P9-CAA-383 "First Thanksgiving" gi settlers in 1621.

The U.S. Army defeated the Japanese and liberated Vietnam in 1945.

V... pe
Péta... the

The ... s the
uninter... airman

Australia was established purely as a penal colony, a dumping ground for Britain's convicts.

Captain Scott: Intrepid Antarctic explorer and iconic British hero.

Bolsheviks, under the charismatic leadership of Lenin, heroically stormed the Winter Palace in the October Revolution of 1917.

A gift for:

_____

Presented by:

_____

History

THEY GOT IT WRONG

History

All the **Facts** That Turned Out to Be **Myths**

Emma Marriott

Reader's
digest

The Reader's Digest Association, Inc.
New York, NY / Montreal

A READER'S DIGEST BOOK

Copyright © Michael O'Mara Books Limited 2013

First published in Great Britain in 2011 by Michael O'Mara Books Limited, 9 Lion Yard, Tremadoc Road, London SW4 7NQ.

Maps and technical drawings by David Woodroofe.
Illustrations by Andrew Pinder.

Library of Congress Cataloging-in-Publication Data
Marriott, Emma.
  They got it wrong, history : all the facts that turned out to be myths / by Emma Marriott.
      p. cm.
  "First published in Great Britain in 2011 by Michael O'Mara Books Limited."
  Includes bibliographical references and index.
  ISBN 978-1-62145-008-5 (alk. paper) -- ISBN 978-1-62145-022-1 (epub)
  1. History--Miscellanea. 2. History--Errors, inventions, etc. I. Title.
  D10.M374 2013
  909--dc23

                        2012035133

ISBN 978-1-62145-008-5 (hardcover)
ISBN 978-1-62145-087-0 (paperback)

We are committed to both the quality of our products and the service we provide to our customers. We value your comments, so please feel free to contact us.

                The Reader's Digest Association, Inc.
                Adult Trade Publishing
                44 South Broadway
                White Plains, NY 10601

For more Reader's Digest products and information, visit our website:
                www.rd.com (in the United States)
                www.readersdigest.ca (in Canada)

Printed in Hong Kong

3 5 7 9 10 8 6 4 2

CONTENTS

∽o∾

The main killing sites of the Holocaust
were Auschwitz and the
concentration camps in Germany.
42

Benito Mussolini made the trains run on time.
50

The defeat of the Spanish Armada was a heroic
victory for the English and the beginning of
their supremacy of the seas.
54

Captain Scott: Intrepid Antarctic explorer
and iconic British hero.
60

French Revolutionary doctor Joseph Guillotin
invented the guillotine.
68

The Man in the Iron Mask was Louis XIV's brother.
74

Australia was established purely as a penal colony, a
dumping ground for Britain's convicts.
81

President Roosevelt's New Deal saved capitalism and
lifted the United States out of the Depression.
90

Abraham Lincoln's main aim in fighting the
Civil War was to free the slaves.

96

The United States entered World War I at the last minute
and contributed little to the Allied victory.

104

The Great Famine in China was the unintentional
consequence of Chairman Mao's economic reforms.

112

James Watt invented the steam engine.

119

The attack on Pearl Harbor was deliberately
engineered by President Roosevelt.

124

The Italian astronomer Galileo was persecuted by the
Catholic Church and imprisoned in a dark cell.

130

Bloody Mary was a ruthless persecutor of
English Protestants.

136

St. Patrick was Irish.

142

Roman gladiators fought to the death.

147

INTRODUCTION

∽o∽

"History is a pack of lies about events that never happened told by people who weren't there."

—George Santayana

The chronicles of history are littered with myths and legends, misinformation, falsehoods, embellishment, wild exaggeration, and a whole lot of confusion. All this makes for an awful lot of "bad" history. As Mr. Santayana says, the problem with history is that we weren't actually there, and we rely on other people who also weren't there to tell us what happened and why. This means that historical "facts"—like the ones drilled into us at school—are not quite what they seem. The best we can say for a lot of them is that they are "probably true," while others—like that Lincoln's main goal of the Civil War was the emancipation of the slaves or that St. Patrick was Irish—turn out to be, well, probably not true.

There are a myriad of reasons why events or people

from the past are misrepresented or misunderstood. Archaeological or documentary evidence may be lacking, unreliable, or bewilderingly inconsistent (ask ten or twenty witnesses what happened at a particular incident, and you'll get ten or twenty different versions). Extrapolating what happened at any given event is a tricky business. If you then add in a large chunk of time, be it a decade or several centuries, some might say it's an almost impossible task.

Problems also arise when we wrench something out of the past and examine it out of context. We can't pretend we don't live in the present, and no matter how much we try, modern sensibilities shape our view of history—and the conclusions that we draw often speak volumes about our own beliefs. In the last century, Captain Scott was revered as a great explorer; now many think of him as an ill-advised fool. Which is it to be? And which is the example of "bad" history?

History, like life, is annoyingly complex (and confusing); so packaging the past into a neat story so that it fits some kind of preconceived notion has its dangers. We liken our historical figures to imaginary characters, and assign to them the familiar stereotypes of either hero or villain. We forget, however, that they were real-life people, who, like us, were probably a combination of good and bad. We much prefer our victories in battle to be resounding and decisive, and not, like many military engagements, muddled, open-ended, and inconsequential. While these embellishments make for exciting stories—we all love a dashing hero or a resounding victory—they also distort the truth, endorse delusions of grandeur, and perpetuate many of the myths with which we are so familiar.

Historical myths, like fairy tales, are generally quite harmless, but when they are seized upon as political weaponry, the consequences can be disastrous. Repressive regimes can cover up a discreditable past or rewrite the history books with their own sanitized version of events (see Chairman Mao on page 112), and propagandists and political leaders can appropriate popular historical myths to lend authority to their own rather dubious belief systems (see Otto von Bismarck on page 25). Conversely, some theorists who are hellbent on proving some kind of government conspiracy or cover-up can also wander into rather sketchy territory (see the attack on Pearl Harbor on page 124).

What follows is an investigation into some of the myths and falsehoods that have become entrenched in popular belief and wrongly influenced our understanding of the world. It is by no means exhaustive—there are without a doubt many more myths out there—but I hope it goes some way to shedding light on some of the worst offenses. Some will disagree with the findings—I too "wasn't there," and, as the historian Pieter Geyl said (at least, I hope he said it), "History is an argument without end." But I'm hoping that the history passed down to us is not *all* a pack of lies, that lurking within what they got wrong are some truths—we just need to keep looking for them.

—Emma Marriott

The Old West was a wild and dangerous place to be.

Few areas of history have gripped the imagination as much as the expansion of the United States into the wilderness of the West. Sensational tales of the "Wild West" portrayed a violent and brutal land where hardy settlers rubbed alongside brave cowboys, ruthless outlaws, and savage Indians, where people took the law into their own hands to protect their families.

This image of the Old West proved hugely popular and was consolidated in folklore, music, and dime novels that sold millions of copies in the second half of the nineteenth century. Soldier and showman Buffalo Bill Cody similarly popularized the legend of the frontier through his Wild West shows. In 1893, Buffalo Bill's show featured a new act of "Rough Riders" consisting of marksmen from all over the world—including future President Theodore Roosevelt.

In the twentieth century, the legend of the Wild West spread to the rest of the world as artists, magazines, and movies spun a whole industry around its mythologization, in which gun-slinging heroes battled against "Injuns" in places where, as Sergio Leone put it, "life has no value." The first Western movie, *The Great Train Robbery*, came out in 1903, and by the 1950s, the genre was also lapped up by television audiences, who could choose from no fewer than twenty-six prime-time Western series in 1959.

Yet the reality of life in the West was quite different from the general lawlessness depicted in the movies. Recent research has shown that crime was relatively low among the West's settlers and that you were more likely to be gunned down in Victorian London than in the Wild West. In the real Dodge City, which at one point was thought of as the biggest and rowdiest town of the Wild West, a total of five deaths in 1878 amounted to the town's worst year for homicides.

Similarly, the legendary shoot-out at the O.K. Corral—a gunfight between two gangs led by Wyatt Earp and Ike Clanton (and regarded as the most famous gun battle in the history of the Old West)— lasted all of sixty seconds and resulted in just three deaths. Face-offs at "high noon" were not common events, and gunfights were usually spontaneous and the result of drunken arguments that had got out of hand. The Wild West mythmakers would also have us believe that bank robberies were everyday events, but Larry Schweikart of the University of Dayton has estimated that between 1859 and 1900 just *twelve* bank robberies occurred along the Western frontier.

Research has also shown that, in the absence of any formal government, settlers devised surprisingly effective ways to protect themselves from all manner of crimes. Voluntary organizations in the form of "wagon-train" governments were set up to police and protect the 300,000 pioneers traveling west to California and Oregon. In the Midwest, land clubs and cattlemen associations settled disputes and enforced property rights. On the West Coast, gold-mining districts set up legal systems that punished crimes against life and property. On the whole, miners avoided violence and abided by the rules of the district. Andrew Morriss of the University of Alabama School of Law writes, "This amazing polyglot of men seeking rapid wealth, and with virtually no intention of building a lasting society, created a set of customary legal institutions which not only flourished in California but successfully adapted to conditions across the West."

MINI MYTH
COWBOYS

Also central to the Wild West myth was the gun-slinging cowboy, the embodiment of the brave lone rider, who, we're led to believe, overran the frontier. In reality, farmers outnumbered cowboys in the West by about a *thousand* to one: there were (at the most) only 10,000 working cowboys, the majority of whom were Hispanic, African-American, or Mexican. Few cowboys could afford a firearm (a modern Colt weapon represented an average nine months' salary), and many died young—not from shoot-outs but from riding accidents or illnesses borne from a hard but decidedly unglamorous life herding cows across vast plains.

Other old West myths, largely popularized by the entertainment industry, include the image of westward migrants lumbering across the Great Plains in Conestoga wagons (large wagons pulled by oxen). In fact, most families used much smaller covered wagons called "prairie schooners," which were hauled by mules or oxen. In addition, wagon trails were not constantly assailed by Native Americans—most pioneers crossed the plains without incident; nor would trails of wagons defend themselves from attacking Indians by maneuvering themselves into galloping circles (the movies borrowed this from the Wild West shows in which limited arena space necessitated the circular formation). Any killings by Native Americans tended to be wildly exaggerated: of the half a million people who passed through Western territories in wagon trains between 1840 and 1860, it's estimated that just 362 died from attacks by hostile natives.

And yet, while bloodshed was relatively low among the West's new settlers, life for America's indigenous population was increasingly brutal. As migrants advanced west, Native Americans were uprooted and moved from their homelands, and many died as a result of war, disease, or loss of livelihood. Between 1830 and 1895 the number of Native Americans fell from 2 million to 90,000, while around 70 million buffalo (the Plains Indians' main source of livelihood) were slaughtered.

The myth of the Wild West has captivated millions across the world and spawned a huge publishing and entertainment industry in the process. In the forging of the new nation of America, exaggerated tales of brave and hardy white men venturing into the unknown have proved far more appealing than the reality of the migrants' grittier, more mundane lives or the brutalities inflicted upon the West's indigenous population. This mythical depiction of the Wild West, perpetuated by Hollywood, was brilliantly satirized by Mel Brooks's 1974 film *Blazing Saddles*, none more so than in Sheriff Bart's farewell to the townspeople of Rock Ridge:

> *Bart:* Work here is done. I'm needed elsewhere now. I'm needed wherever outlaws rule the West, wherever innocent women and children are afraid to walk the streets, wherever a man cannot live in simple dignity, wherever a people cry out for justice.
>
> *Crowd:* [in unison] BULLSHIT!
>
> *Bart:* All right, you caught me. Speaking the plain truth is getting pretty damn dull around here.

I'd give you a belly full of lead, if only I could afford a gun.

REALITY CHECK

NATIVE AMERICAN CUSTOMS

Western movies and popular novels got it wrong: Native Americans did not greet each other with "how." Similarly, "Paleface" and "Great White Father" were the invention of novelists like James Fenimore Cooper (*The Last of the Mohicans*). Indians did not send coded messages to other tribes via smoke signals, nor was scalping a common practice (though it was actually introduced by the white settler). The Native American showed as little concern for their environment as their white counterpart, reducing the population of beavers and the white-tailed deer to near extinction. The image of the Native Americans as the original environmentalist largely stems from a much-quoted 1854 speech by Suquamish Chief Seattle: ". . . the earth does not belong to man—man belongs to the earth. . . ." However, it's possible that these words bear no relation to those actually spoken by Chief Seattle, as he delivered the speech in the language of Lushootseed, which was simultaneously translated into Chinook Jargon. A Dr. Henry Smith reproduced the speech from memory in 1887, and various adaptations have appeared ever since.

The Founding Fathers sought to replace monarchy with democracy.

The U.S. Constitution, written in 1787 in Philadelphia, established the foundation of the government as we know it today—the two legislative houses of Congress (the House of Representatives and Senate), the executive branch of the presidency, and the judicial arm of the Supreme Court. As the Constitution provided the framework for representative democracy in the United States, it seems only reasonable to presume that the Founding Fathers—the men who wrote the Constitution—intended to establish a nation based upon democratic principles.

In reality, the Founding Fathers—which included such luminaries as Benjamin Franklin and George Washington—were wholly united in their opposition to and mistrust of democracy. For them, and for many of their contemporaries, democracy equaled mob rule and anarchy, and the word itself had somewhat dubious associations. The fifty-five delegates who devised and worded the Constitution were largely members of the gentry and lawyers, and a third of them had served in Washington's army. While showing a great deal of intellect and foresight, they shared a conservative outlook and were not shy in voicing their hostility towards democracy. Delegate Edmund Randolph spoke of the "follies and turbulence of democracy," while Roger Sherman said that "the people immediately should have as little to do as may be about the Government."

MINI MYTH

INSIDE GEORGE WASHINGTON'S HEAD

One of the most prevalent myths about George Washington is that he was outfitted with wooden teeth. It is true that he was plagued by bad teeth through his life, as well as many other health ailments. By the time he was inaugurated he only had one original tooth left in his head, but his dentures were far fancier than some whittled, wooden choppers. The day he became the first president, he wore dentures made from elephant and hippopotamus ivory, human teeth, and gold. This set of false teeth was spring-loaded to keep them in place. Perhaps this explains why he never smiled in a portrait.

Although the delegates favored a government that represented the people—and the right of any white freeman of voting age to vote was already very broad-minded when compared to the rest of the world—their intention was to set up an administration that would limit how much citizens could directly participate in national government. Many of the Founding Fathers advocated strict limitations and checks on the "democratic parts" of the Constitution, and almost all of them envisioned a nation ruled by propertied gentlemen.

At one stage, delegate Alexander Hamilton suggested that members of the Senate and the president be elected for life and given absolute power over the states. And following George Washington's rather grand ceremonial inauguration, Congress actually considered altering his title to the more impressive-sounding "His Highness," "His Mightiness," or "His Supremacy," until they backtracked to the less majestic-sounding "President."

In the end, the delegates made one concession to democracy by allowing members of the House of Representatives to be elected by the people (the "people" being white, male property owners). Members of the Senate, however, would be elected by the state legislature, as would the presidency. (It wasn't until 1913 that senators would be elected by popular vote, and we still have the Electoral College today.)

The word democracy continued to be avoided decades after 1787. Thomas Jefferson didn't include it in any public addresses as president, and it wasn't until the twentieth century—after Woodrow Wilson became the first president to do so in a public statement during World War I—that U.S. politicians generally referred to the nation as a democracy.

Since the adoption of the Constitution, a further twenty-seven amendments have broadened the electorate and led to the democratization of U.S. politics. These amendments have largely dismantled the limitations specifically incorporated by the Founding Fathers, whose ideas about political representation were mainly rooted in the colonial past.

His Mightiness
King George

MINI MYTH

THE UNITED STATES OF GERMANY

It is frequently stated with conviction that Congress considered making German the official language of America, a plan that was rejected by just one vote. This is, however, a myth, as no such proposal was ever considered by any legislative body of the U.S. government. Indeed, around ninety percent of the United States' 3.9 million inhabitants spoke English. In 1795, the House of Representatives briefly considered a proposal that all laws and regulations be published in English and German (for the benefit of German citizens who could not speak English). It was never a popular motion, and a vote to adjourn and sit again on the recommendation was rejected by one vote. A month later, it was again raised in the House of Representatives and was immediately and resoundingly rejected. Other similar myths include that the writer Kingsley Amis claimed that Congress voted on establishing Ancient Greek and then an American Indian language, the official language of America—again, not true.

The "Iron Chancellor" Otto von Bismarck: Ruthless, war-mongering conservative and dogmatic ideologue.

Prussian-born Otto von Bismarck is considered the founder of the German Empire, a man who from 1862 to 1890 shaped the fortunes of Germany, first as Minister-President of Prussia and then as Chancellor of the newly established German Empire. For decades after his death in 1898, Bismarck was venerated as a national hero, the "most German of all Germans." But when his image was used to legitimize the far-right politics that came to plague Germany in the 1930s and 1940s, Bismarck's legacy took a real battering and led to the demonization of him as a ruthless, ultra-conservative despot, who paved the way for the Nazi regime.

Having achieved a series of Prussian victories in Europe, Bismarck secured in 1871 the political unification of German states and, with the European power balance radically altered, skillfully maintained peace through a series of European alliances. At home, he set up a national currency and initiated a common code of German law, while also implementing a number of laws designed to severely limit the influence of the left-wing Social Democratic Party and the Catholic Church.

Although always a staunch conservative and opponent of liberalism, Bismarck was not a dogmatic ideologue, nor was he fixated on war in Europe. Indeed, in foreign affairs, he developed into a master of diplomacy, and the conduct of foreign affairs became one of his main preoccupations throughout his chancellorship. He purposely *avoided* war by maintaining an elaborate and constantly shifting system of political alliances in Europe that were aimed at isolating France (which remained a bitter enemy of Germany). At home, his intent was to build a powerful German Reich (Empire) and develop a national consciousness, and while he attacked Catholicism and Socialism in pursuit of this, he did personally reject anti-Semitism and viewed radical nationalism as a threat to the peace and security of the German Empire.

After Bismarck's resignation in 1890 and death in 1898, conservatives and liberals alike mythologized him as the "Iron Chancellor," a ruthless promoter of the policy of "Blood and Iron," referring to his speech of 1862: "Not by speeches and majority decisions are the great questions of the day decided — that was the great error of 1848 and 1849 — but by iron and blood." As Kaiser Wilhelm II's popularity declined during the 1920s, Bismarck was increasingly revered as the man who had laid the foundations of Germany's "greatness," whose strong leadership contrasted sharply with the weakness of parliamentary rule. He was to become one of the most popular German statesmen of all time.

As Robert Gerwarth describes in *The Bismarck Myth*, the myth built up around Bismarck was useful for future leaders and politicians in Germany, but it would lead to a false image of who he really was and what he did for his country.

Kaiser Wilhelm II first used Bismarck's reputation to justify Germany's expansionist policies overseas

REALITY CHECK
A COMPLEX CHARACTER

The crude stereotype of Bismarck as a "power politician in soldier's boots" bears little relation to his more complex character. Bismarck's appearance seemed to fit the indomitable image—he usually wore his uniform in public, although he had only one very inglorious year of military service, which he did not enjoy—whereas his temperament seemed more artistic and high strung, earning him the name of "wild Bismarck" in his twenties. Later in life, he would often resort to tantrums and crying fits to get his way with his sovereign. His public speeches were not the rants of a megalomaniac but were carefully worded (they still read well today), and he delighted in using sarcasm and irony.

(although Bismarck had originally opposed the acquisition of foreign colonies, considering them too expensive) while attacking those who opposed the social order of Germany as a crime against the legacy of the Iron Chancellor. After World War I and the subsequent humiliation of the German state, Bismarck served as a reminder of what Germany had lost. Mounting dissatisfaction with the Weimer Republic, along with the

worldwide Great Depression after 1929, further inten-
sified the desire for a strong and charismatic leader, a
"second Bismarck" who could solve Germany's problems and reassert its former greatness.

The adulation of Bismarck also gave an emerging
style of right-wing politics a historical legitimacy. Adolf
Hitler evoked the memory of Bismarck and Frederick
the Great, and presented himself as the only man able
to continue their legacies, declaring in January of 1931
that "if Bismarck were to return with his political comrades, they would all stand on our side today." However,
once Hitler's regime was established in 1933, the public veneration of Bismarck faded. The Nazis could not
allow the greatness of past leaders to overshadow that
of Adolf Hitler. For this reason, as Robert Gerwarth in
History Today noted, public Bismarck celebrations were
declared illegal in Germany.

The mythologization of Bismarck (and its appro-
priation by future leaders) ultimately proved disastrous for Germany, although the vast disparities between Hitler—a reckless gambler and demagogue
who brought ruin to Germany—and Bismarck—a
cautious political player, but a gambler when he
needed to be—are clear. In 1944, when Germany's
defeat was imminent, Ulrich von Hassell, who had

previously not been Bismarck's greatest proponent, lamented:

> It is regrettable, what a false picture of him we ourselves have given the world—that of a power politician in soldier's boots—in our childish joy over the fact that at least someone had made Germany a name to reckon with again. In his own way he knew how to win confidence in the world; exactly the reverse of what is done today. In truth, the highest diplomacy and great moderation were his real gifts.

REALITY CHECK
BISMARCK: ADORED OR ABHORRED?

Bismarck received far more adulation after his resignation and death than he ever did as Chancellor. His shifting foreign policy and his anti-Catholicism and anti-Socialism had created distrust within the political culture of Germany. However, he abandoned his anti-Catholic stance in the 1880s, and, despite Bismarck's disapproval, the Socialists continued to flourish so that by 1914 they were the biggest party in the Reichstag. The German press expressed little grief over Bismarck's resignation, and his departure from Berlin was accompanied by cheering crowds. The novelist Theodor Fontane even wrote in a letter, "It is good fortune that we finally got rid of him."

Bolsheviks, under the charismatic leadership of Lenin, heroically stormed the Winter Palace in the October Revolution of 1917.

The October Revolution of 1917, which followed the February Revolution of the same year, saw the Bolsheviks seize power in Russia. Bolshevik Red Guards began the takeover of key buildings in Petrograd (St. Petersburg) on the night of October 24–25, 1917, and finally captured the Winter Palace, the seat of Russia's Provisional Government, the following night. "Official" histories, paintings, novels, and films have depicted the storming of the Winter Palace as part of a mass rising, in which large numbers fought fiercely to break into a heavily guarded palace, yet the reality of the Russian Revolution was far less dramatic.

Indeed, this depiction of events is, as the historian

Steve Phillips puts it in *Lenin and the Russian Revolution,* "a gross exaggeration." Much of it is based on "politically correct" accounts created by Bolshevik propagandists, whose intention was to portray the events of October 1917 as a heroic and dramatic struggle. This was reinforced by an official historical reenactment shown to 100,000 spectators on the third anniversary of the revolution. Entitled *The Storming of the Winter Palace,* it depicted a huge siege and fierce battle. Later films portrayed a similar image, significantly Sergei Eisenstein's *October: Ten Days That Shook the World,* a documentary-style movie made in 1927, which showed Bolshevik leader Lenin and thousands of Red Guards storming the palace. So authentic did this movie seem to be that for years television documentaries passed off this particular scene as actual "footage" from the revolution.

Free from official Soviet biases, Western historians have portrayed the revolution in numerous ways, and many have debunked the heroic myth of a large-scale struggle. Indeed, the real events of October were far less dramatic: by the time the Bolsheviks entered the Winter Palace, it was virtually unoccupied. Its gates were open; its administrative staff and many of its guards had fled; and the few that remained had barricaded themselves in the former private rooms of the imperial family. The provisional government had by this time little support in the city and so little power that, as Steve Phillips remarks in *Lenin and the Russian Revolution*, "it was hardly worth overthrowing."

General Knox, a British military attaché in Russia, observed the taking of the palace:

> The garrison of the Winter Palace originally consisted of about 2,000 all told . . . The garrison dwindled owing to desertions . . . No one had any stomach for fighting; and some of the ensigns even borrowed great coats of soldier pattern from any women to enable them to escape unobserved . . . At 10 p.m., a large part of the ensigns left, leaving few defenders except the ensigns of the Engineering School and the company of women. [The so-called Women's Death Battalions.]

American-born journalist and socialist John Reed also witnessed the siege and wrote in his book *Ten Days That Shook the World* (on which Eisenstein's film was based) that by 2 a.m., once Bolshevik insurgents had flooded into the building, "there was no violence done although the Junkers [students] were terrified." Such was the mammoth and heroic storming of the symbol of czardom: the Winter Palace.

Cultural depictions of Vladimir Lenin and his role in the events of October 17 have also been misrepresented. Contrary to popular belief, he did not lead the Bolshevik troops into the palace, nor did he spur on the insurgents with a string of public speeches (as depicted in films, novels, and even ballets with "fist raised, mouth tensed and a bearded chin"). On that particular day, Lenin—who, incidentally, had no beard at this time in an attempt to disguise himself from the authorities—spoke only briefly at the Second Congress and acted more as a strategist and, as Robert Service notes in *Lenin*, an "inspirer behind the scenes."

It's estimated that only six people lost their lives in Petrograd during the October Revolution, of whom none were defenders of the existing government. Unlike the February Revolution—during which roughly 1,500 people died and hundreds of thousands were out on the streets protesting—this was not a mass uprising. The Winter Palace was not "stormed" by thousands of troops, but simply walked into by a much smaller group of fairly disorganized soldiers, who faced little or no opposition.

REALITY CHECK

LEON TROTSKY: HERO OR TRAITOR?

The military force needed to overthrow the Provisional Government in Petrograd was largely orchestrated by Leon Trotsky, not Lenin. Trotsky had joined the Bolsheviks just prior to the October Revolution. As chairman of the Soviet Petrograd, he had set up the Military Revolutionary Committee, which took over the capital's garrison and city a week before the uprising, leaving just the Winter Palace holding out on the night of October 24–25. On November 10, 1918, Stalin wrote in the newspaper *Pravda*:

> All practical work in connection with the organization of the uprising was done under the immediate direction of Comrade Trotsky, the President of the Petrograd Soviet. It can be stated with certainty that the Party is indebted primarily and principally to Comrade Trotsky for the rapid going over of the garrison to the side of the Soviet and the efficient manner in which the work of the Military Revolutionary Committee was organized.

A somewhat ironic statement considering Stalin would later hound and hunt Trotsky to his death.

Christopher Columbus introduced syphilis to Europe.

It is a commonly believed that the Italian explorer Christopher Columbus introduced syphilis to Europe. Following his historic voyage to the Americas in 1492, it was thought that Columbus's crew had picked up the unfamiliar disease of syphilis from the Americas and brought it back to Europe the next year. However, recent discoveries have shown that syphilis may well have existed in Europe long before Columbus first set foot in the New World (and maybe the transmission of the disease went the other way around).

The theory of Columbus's culpability is not without foundation, though, as the earliest-known European epidemic of syphilis broke out in 1494 or 1495, soon after Columbus's return. The disease struck French troops in Naples during their invasion of Italy, and documentary evidence cites links between the French army and crewmen of the Columbus voyage. Syphilis went on to ravage Europe and led to an estimated 5 million deaths. In an era without antibiotics, it was a fearsome disease that caused serious damage to its victim's skin, joints, stomach, heart, and brain, leading to death within a few months.

In 2008, *New Scientist* magazine reported on evidence that supported the Columbus link. Findings indicated that the sexually transmitted form of syphilis had originated more recently, suggesting that Europeans could have picked up a non-venereal form of the disease, which then mutated into a more deadly, sexually transmittable form. In addition, upon examination, the venereal-causing strains of syphilis appeared to be closely related to those found in South America (where Columbus and his crew landed).

However, even more recent evidence has established the existence of syphilis in Europe long before the voyage of 1492. In east London, on the excavation site of one of the largest medieval hospitals, osteologists like Brian Connell have unearthed skeletons dating from 1200 to 1400 that show clear signs of the syphilis disease. Out of 5,387 skeletons examined, a total of twenty-five show the terrible bone damage inflicted by the condition. One skeleton belonged to a ten-year-old child, who, experts believe, was born with the infection and whose remains showed the painful, disfiguring symptoms characteristic of its later stages. Syphilitic lesions had caused dents in the child's skull, and the child's canine teeth protruded at a forty-five-degree angle. Brian Connell said, "It caused a bit of stir when it was found because the symptoms are so obvious."

REALITY CHECK
TRUE AFFLICTIONS

Columbus's voyage to the Americas in 1492 launched an era of wide-scale contact between the New and Old Worlds, known as "The Columbian Exchange" (a term coined by historian Alfred W. Crosby). New foods and crops (including tobacco), animals, ideas, and people (often in the form of slaves) were exchanged, as were a host of deadly diseases. European afflictions, which included influenza and smallpox, decimated the population of the Americas, and it has been estimated that between 1492 and 1650, the indigenous population of the Americas declined from 50 million to 5 million. Thus, for many people in the Americas, Columbus kick-started a rapid decline in population with genocidal effect.

Recent discoveries in the ruins of Pompeii also indicate the presence of syphilis in early Europe. The remains of twin children who died in the eruption of Mount Vesuvius in 79 CE have been found to show almost certainly the signs of congenital (hereditary) syphilis. Some experts believe that Hippocrates described the symptoms of venereal syphilis in ancient Greece, which means the disease may have been around over four hundred years even before the volcanic destruction of Pompeii. In addition, skeletons of monks who lived at a thirteenth- to fourteenth-century Augustinian friary in Kingston-upon-Hull in England showed bone lesions indicative of venereal syphilis.

Douglas Owsley, an anthropologist at the Smithsonian Institution, also put forward the idea that syphilis had existed in both hemispheres before 1492 but was mistaken in the medieval period for leprosy—it is simply coincidental that the mistaken leprosy symptoms flared up in virulence at the end of the fifteenth century. Other molecular geneticists have argued that it's likely syphilis emerged in Europe spontaneously, possibly from related bacteria already rife in the Old World.

Although the first known European epidemic of syphilis broke out in the immediate aftermath of

MINI MYTH

THE COLUMBUS DISCOVERY

Columbus was once thought of as the "discoverer" of America, even though the indigenous people had been there for thousands of years and the Vikings had settled there several centuries earlier. What also tends to be forgotten is that Columbus never actually set foot in North America, as his four voyages took him to the Caribbean and the coast of South America. Added to that, when he first reached Cuba, he insisted that it was part of the Asian mainland and thus named its inhabitants "indios" ("Indians").

For almost three hundred years after his voyages, Columbus was largely forgotten, until post-revolutionary Americans, in their search for heroes unconnected with the British monarchy, resurrected his memory. In the 1930s President Franklin D. Roosevelt (partly in a bid to please Italian Americans, who were important supporters of his party) revived the myth and established the Columbus Day public holiday. The spirit of Columbus ran through all Americans, Roosevelt maintained: "You are scarcely removed one generation from men and women who [. . .] sought to conquer nature for the benefit of the Nation."

Columbus's historic voyage, he was not responsible for bringing the disease to Europe. New evidence suggests syphilis had been present in Europe as early as the first century CE, and therefore the man who was once credited as being the first European to reach the Americas (another case where they got it wrong—see facing page)—and who may have instigated the exchange of a host of other diseases between the Old and New Worlds (see box on page 38)—has finally been exonerated.

The main killing sites of the Holocaust were Auschwitz and the concentration camps in Germany.

For most people around the world, the image of the Holocaust centers upon Auschwitz and the German concentration camps. These are seen as the main killing sites of the Jews in Europe—mass murder achieved on an industrial scale, largely by means of the gas chamber. Memoirs, photographs, historic books, and news footage portray the appalling images with which we are now familiar, and these now stand as testament to one of the worst atrocities of the twentieth century.

Auschwitz was built in German-occupied Poland and served as both a concentration camp and an extermination camp. It became Nazi Germany's main

REALITY CHECK
THE CAMPS

The term "concentration camp" has been used synonymously for all types of camps established by Nazi Germany, but there was a distinct difference between the *concentration* camp and the *extermination* camp. The former were set up as places of incarceration, and the latter were established for the sole purpose of industrial-scale mass murder. As Timothy Snyder in his groundbreaking book *Blood Lands* writes, "The concentration camps did kill hundreds of thousands of people at the end of the war, but they were not (in contrast to the death facilities) designed for mass killing."

extermination site by 1944, and approximately one sixth of the 5.7 million Jews killed in the Holocaust died there from February 1943 through the end of the war. And yet Auschwitz and the German concentration camps formed just one aspect of an appallingly intricate network of camps and directives designed by the Nazis to exterminate the European Jewish population and others that they deemed unfit for life.

As Timothy Snyder writes, "Mass killing in Europe

Nazi death and concentration camps

is usually associated with the Holocaust, and the Holocaust with rapid industrial killing. The image is too simple and clean." In reality, the Germans utilized a host of other primitive methods of killing across German-occupied lands (and much of it outside of the extermination camps), from starvation and forced labor to impromptu executions and mass shootings.

The German occupation of Poland in 1939 swelled the number of Jewish people under Nazi control from around 300,000 (200,000 of which were German Jews, just one percent of the German population) to around 2 million. After invasion, Polish civilians (Jewish and non-Jewish alike) were shot by the thousands by killing squads called *Einsatzgruppen*, and starting in 1940, ghettos were set up as a form of holding pens and labor camps for the Jewish population until they could be transported elsewhere. In 1940, more than 100,000 Jews were moved into the Warsaw ghetto, of which around 60,000 would die as a result of starvation or deprivation.

With Germany gaining control of the Baltic States and the western Soviet Union in 1941, a total of some 5 million Jewish people were under the control of the Reich. In the same year, Hitler gave Heinrich Himmler and Hermann Goering the order to exterminate all

Jews. By August 1941 mass shootings in areas east of the Molotov-Ribbentrop Line (mainly eastern Poland, Lithuania, Latvia, Estonia, and the western Soviet States, see map on facing page) escalated to horrific proportions. The Einsatzgruppen, often enlisting local policemen and officials, oversaw many of the shootings, and further SS reinforcements were sent in so that entire communities of men, women, and children could be annihilated.

In September 1941, as an act of reprisal for a bombing that had killed occupying Germans in Kiev, all Jews were ordered to gather at a certain point in the city, having been given the standard lie that they were to be resettled. Instead, they were driven to the edge of the Babi Yar ravine and shot, each person ordered to lie down on the long line of mounting corpses before they themselves were gunned down. The whole process took thirty-six hours, and 33,761 people lost their lives. By the end of 1941, around one million Jews had been killed in this manner.

Mass shooting of civilians continued throughout 1942, and gas vans, first tested on Soviet POWs, were also utilized throughout German-occupied lands. West of the Molotov-Ribbentrop Line, gassing facilities were implemented, and in Poland the extermination camps of Bełżec, Sobibor, and Treblinka were set up. These relatively unknown camps, established to fulfill the Reinhard Action (named after Reinhard Heydrich, a Gestapo chief), were built purely for the purposes of murder (and were thus distinct from German concentration camps, such as Belsen and Dachau, which were designed primarily for slave labor and incarceration). Together with Chelmno, the Reinhard death camps went on to kill around 1.5 million Jews.

A map showing the Molotov-Ribbentrop Line, established in August 1939

Whereas around 100,000 people survived Auschwitz, virtually no one who entered the death camps of Bełżec, Sobibor, or Treblinka came out alive. The survivors of Auschwitz lived to speak of the horror of their experiences, whereas few people even knew of the existence of the Reinhard death camps because so few inmates survived. At the end of the war, American and British forces liberated German concentration camps, but they did not visit or witness the death facilities of Poland (some of which were liberated by the Red Army; others, including Bełżec, Sobibor, and Treblinka, were demolished by the Nazis). Thus little was known about some of the Reinhard extermination camps, despite the huge numbers killed there (434,508 Jews were killed at Bełżec alone).

While Auschwitz was a major site of the Holocaust, by the time it had been set up, three-quarters of the Jews killed (and almost all of the biggest Jewish communities: the Polish and Soviet Jews) had already died. The majority of Jews killed didn't see a concentration camp and the atrocities committed in Auschwitz, and the concentration camps of Nazi Germany did not represent the full horror of the Holocaust. In reality, the main killing sites were to be found in the extermination camps and across German-occupied lands, where civilians were slaughtered by the millions.

REALITY CHECK
THE BRUTALITY OF AUSCHWITZ

Most Jews who arrived at Auschwitz were gassed immediately. A minority were selected for labor and worked to exhaustion before being gassed. In addition, some 200,000 of Auschwitz's victims were not Jews—74,000 being non-Jewish Poles and 15,000 Soviets. Only at Auschwitz were all inmates tattooed with an identification number. Formerly, inmates had had their numbers sewn into their clothes, and they could be shot if they didn't remember their number. The tattooing practice began in spring 1943, by use of a large metal stamp comprising several needles forced into the upper left chest. Beginning in 1944, numbers were tattooed on to the left forearm.

Benito Mussolini made the trains run on time.

"At least the trains ran on time under Mussolini." That is a statement frequently uttered by exasperated commuters or those trying to make the point that even brutal dictators have their good points. Unfortunately, they've fallen for Fascist propaganda, as Mussolini didn't make the trains run on time (nor did he have many good points).

The Italian rail network had fallen into a parlous state during the First World War, and improvements were made to it in the 1920s and 1930s with the electrification of lines, the enhancement of rolling stock, and the building of main routes between Rome and Naples, and between Bologna and Florence (which included the building of the second-longest tunnel in the world, opened with triumphant fanfare as "building Fascism"). Peter Neville in *Mussolini*, however, maintains that much of the groundwork for these improvements had already been put in place by the time Mussolini came to power. Mussolini's government benefited from recently established stock and relatively uncongested lines, and simply took the credit for many improvements initiated by previous administrations.

In 1936, American journalist George Seldes wrote that the trains more commonly used by tourists on the main express lines usually arrived on time but those on smaller lines were frequently late. Other testimonies from the period suggest that even the trains on the bigger lines were often delayed. The British journalist Elizabeth Wiskemann dismissed the "myth about the punctual trains . . . I traveled in a number that were late," she wrote.

The notion that Italy's trains ran on time was largely created by the propaganda machine set up by the Fascist authorities. Mussolini's key priority in government was to subjugate the hearts and minds of the Italian people, and to impress on them and the wider world the benefits of Fascism versus the doctrines of liberalism or democracy. The press, radio, films, and educational programs went into overdrive as the new government pushed through various initiatives, often dubbing reforms as "battles" (such as the marsh reclamation project, which was hailed as the "Battle for Land").

REALITY CHECK
THE ORIGINS OF EFFICIENCY

Mussolini came to power in 1922. In a bid to win over the Italian public, he drew attention to the myth of Fascist efficiency, using the Italian train services as its symbol. Addressing a stationmaster, he is quoted as saying, "We must leave exactly on time. . . . From now on everything must function to perfection." Word soon spread that Mussolini had turned Italy's dilapidated old railway system into one that was the envy of the world. Infanta Eulalia of Spain wrote in her 1925 book *Courts and Countries After the War*, "The first benefit of Benito Mussolini's direction in Italy begins to be felt when one crosses the Italian frontier and hears 'Il treno arriva orario.'" (The train is arriving on time.)

In the same way, Mussolini used the rail industry to illustrate the effectiveness of his rule. George Seldes wrote, "Official press agents and official philosophers . . . explained to the world that the running of trains was the symbol of the restoration of law and order." The new government also took care to ban the reporting of all railway accidents and delays, thereby cementing the myth of train punctuality.

This myth has outstanding durability, largely because it seems to illustrate how something good can come out of the very worst circumstances. It was a view that similarly infuriated George Seldes, who complained in 1936 about fellow countrymen holidaying in Italy who when they returned to the United States seemed to cry in unison, "Great is the Duce, the trains now run on time." And no matter how often they were told about Fascist oppression, injustice, and cruelty, they always said the same thing: "But the trains run on time."

WRONG

The defeat of the Spanish Armada was a heroic victory for the English and the beginning of their supremacy of the seas.

In 1588, the vast fleet of the Spanish Armada set sail for England. At the behest of its Catholic king, Philip II, the Spanish convoy aimed to invade England, remove Elizabeth I from the throne, and thereby put an end to her piratical raids on Spanish ships and support of Protestant rebels in the Spanish-controlled Netherlands. A heroic battle ensued in which a smaller but more nimble convoy of English ships hounded and outwitted the huge Spanish fleet, eventually forcing it up the east coast of England and into the Atlantic Ocean.

The defeat of the Spanish Armada has generated a great deal of myth and confusion, much of it borne from the common perception that the battle represented a "stunning underdog" victory for the English, who were vastly "outnumbered and outgunned" by the Spanish fleet. In fact, the English had a greater number of better-equipped vessels in the water than the invading fleet, and had the erratic British weather, among other things, on their side.

As the Spanish Armada lay moored off Calais, unable to regroup with additional forces from the Low Countries, the English set fire to several old ships and sent them crashing into the Spanish fleet.

REALITY CHECK
A Numbers Game

The Spanish fleet consisted of about 130 ships, most of which were troop-carrying vessels bearing 19,000 infantrymen under the command of the inexperienced Duke of Medina Sidonia. A minority of the Spanish ships, perhaps as few as thirty-five, were designed for warfare, with only nineteen of these fighting ships suited to the Atlantic waters. While the Spanish had bigger, bulkier ships, the English confronted its adversary with a greater number of vessels that were smaller but more nimble and easier to maneuver.

In the ensuing Battle of Gravelines, the English gained the upper hand, largely by means of cannons that could fire at long distances and rapidly reload when closer in. The English lost no ships, and while it's frequently claimed the Spanish fleet suffered severe damage, in reality they lost just three ships, whose seaworthiness was probably already in question. Lack of ammunition and worsening weather forced the English fleet to break off hostilities, and the Armada was able to escape, in historian Felipe Fernández-Armesto's words, "essentially intact and effectively undefeated, scotched but not killed, bloodied but unbowed."

Strong winds then forced Medina Sidonia to order the Armada—still at this point a formidable fleet of ships, capable of sea warfare—to return to Spain and Portugal via the tip of Scotland and Ireland. Storms— not English cannon—led to the sinking of numerous Spanish vessels as severe storms pushed them onto the rocky coasts of Scotland and Ireland. While it was once thought that the majority of the Spanish fleet were lost in the Atlantic waters, Fernández-Armesto maintains that only twenty-one ships were sunk and that up to five-sixths of the Spanish convoy returned home, with most of the main fighting ships intact.

These events of 1588 were almost immediately mythologized by English writers, who likened the repulse of the Spanish navy as the greatest English victory since Agincourt. The battle came to grip the national consciousness, while seeming to give strength to the Protestant cause in Europe. God himself had favored what was seen as a moral English victory over the spiritually degenerate Spanish. Commemorative medals were issued, one with the inscription, "He blew with His winds, and they were scattered."

The scale of the English victory was monumentalized as a battle of David and Goliath proportions when, as early as a few weeks after the battle, Thomas Deloney penned three ballads that described the Spanish fleet as having "great Galleazzo,/which was so huge and hye" compared to the "little Barkes" of the English. This depiction of the battle actually grew in potency so that even today the disparity between the might of the Spanish and English fleets is often overemphasized.

It's also commonly believed that the 1588 victory over the Spanish Armada saw the beginning of England's dominance over the seas. What tends to be forgotten is that the defeat of the Spanish Armada was just one of many sea and land battles fought during the

Anglo-Spanish War between 1585 and 1604. Spain recovered quickly from the 1588 confrontation, rebuilt and retooled its navy (making subsequent vessels more nimble and effective), and defeated England in several military and naval engagements over the next decade. In 1589 an English Armada launched against the Spanish navy which resulted in total failure and heavy English casualties. In 1596 and 1597 Spain launched more Armadas against the English, but adverse weather conditions continued to protect the British Isles from invasion. The Anglo-Spanish war ended in a stalemate, but Spanish possessions in Europe and the Americas remained intact while efficient convoys of Spanish ships safeguarded and even expanded its lucrative trade route of precious metals from the Americas. Spain's victories at sea continued and were not seriously reversed until the 1630s, while England's maritime strength grew slowly and haltingly. By the late 1600s, the Dutch overtook Spain as the leading sea power, and it wasn't until the mid-1700s that England truly ruled the waves.

The defeat of the Spanish Armada was in no way decisive, except in myth, and the size of the Spanish fleet and its losses are often vastly exaggerated. In the decade following 1588, Spain strengthened its navy and bolstered its overseas possessions, whereas England failed to capitalize on her early victory, had at this point no real foothold in the Americas, and was again saved by the adverse weather—or "Protestant wind"—of the Atlantic waters, which thwarted subsequent Spanish invasion.

Captain Scott: Intrepid Antarctic explorer and iconic British hero.

British Antarctic explorer Captain Robert Falcon Scott, once seen as the quintessential British hero beloved of schoolboys across the land, has become the subject of bitter controversy. His iconic status as intrepid explorer, whose story captured the public's imagination for some sixty years after his death in 1912, came under sustained attack in the 1970s when closer examination of his polar expedition revealed that he was in fact a "heroic bungler" who led his comrades to their deaths.

Captain Scott's ill-fated *Terra Nova* Expedition into the Antarctic set off in 1910 with the expressed objective to be the first expedition to "reach the South Pole, and to secure for the British Empire the honor of this achievement." On January 17, 1912, Scott and his four companions reached the South Pole only to discover that a Norwegian party led by Roald Amundsen had beat them there just under five weeks earlier. The 850-mile return journey—which Scott feared would be "dreadfully tiring and monotonous"—ended in disaster as one by one the team perished from a combination of frostbite, starvation, and exhaustion, with Scott himself probably dying last on or around March 29, 1912.

The frozen bodies of Scott and two other members of the team were discovered the following November,

REALITY CHECK
A "MESSAGE TO THE PUBLIC"

Scott's records included a "Message to the Public"—written primarily as a defense of the team's actions—that ended with the rousing words:

Had we lived, I should have had a tale to tell of the hardihood, endurance and courage of my companions which would have stirred the heart of every Englishman. These rough notes and our dead bodies must tell the tale, but surely, surely, a great rich country like ours will see that those who are dependent on us are properly provided for.

along with Scott's own letters and journals in which he had provided a powerful and harrowing account of the doomed expedition. Scott described how Captain Oates, with his leg frostbitten and gangrenous, uttered the immortal words, "I am just going outside and may be some time," before walking into a blizzard and certain death.

News of Scott and his men's deaths, combined with a memorial service in St. Paul's Cathedral and the publication of his diaries at the end of 1913, had a huge impact on the British public. Although there was little interest in Scott before he left for the Antarctic (Ernest Shackleton was the preferred hero of the time), reports of his demise led to an immense outpouring of public grief as newspapers ran glowing tributes, and over the next dozen years monuments and memorials were set up around the country.

The expedition of Scott—a story driven by the virtues of endurance, stoicism, and suffering—aroused a strong nationalist spirit in the British people. The end of World War I served to increase the desire for a national hero, and the 1922 publication of *The Worst Journey in the World* by Apsley Cherry-Garrard (one of the team who had discovered the bodies of Scott and his two companions) kept the memory of Scott alive. The 1948 film release of *Scott of the Antarctic*, in which Sir John Mills portrays Scott as a classic, stiff-upper-lipped hero, further established his legendary status for years to come.

In 1979, however, Scott's heroic standing came under serious scrutiny with the publication of Roland Huntford's book *Scott and Amundsen (The Last Place on Earth)*. Having examined in detail records from both the British and Norwegian expeditions, Huntford showed how Scott had failed in even the most basic principles of polar expedition. Not only did his lack of food supplies lead to the dehydration and malnutrition of the team, but also his equipment was inappropriate for the extreme weather. While Amundsen's use of skis and ski champions, dogs (more than 200 and with expert dog drivers), and sleds was an efficient combination, Scott's use of skis, dogs (just thirty-five), ponies (which were unsuited to the extreme weather), sleds, and man-hauling (which Scott believed was less cruel than using animals, and somehow more noble) ultimately led to the deaths of all five men. In his extensive research, Huntford discovered Scott to be, in fact, a man who was disorganized, inflexible, overly sentimental, and self-absorbed. The hero was toppled.

More recent writers have sought to rescue Scott's reputation, in particular the polar explorer Sir Ranulph Fiennes who in his 2003 book *Captain Scott* vehemently dismissed Huntford's findings and described Scott as a great historic hero. Susan Solomon, in her research of the meteorological data in 1912, also put forward the theory that extreme weather conditions were to blame for Scott's failure. However Huntford's latest book *Race for the South Pole: The Expedition Diaries of Scott and Amundsen* contains the unedited diaries of

REALITY CHECK
THE BENEFITS OF FUR

The Norwegian team was much better prepared for the extreme weather of the Antarctic. Amundsen had learned from the Eskimos on the North-West Passage to use fur clothing and loose-fitting inner and outer garments to create air pockets and better air circulation. The British team shunned the use of fur—which was not deemed acceptable for civilized men due to its association with primitive tribes—and instead used anoraks with separate hoods.

Scott, with the cuts that had been carefully excised from earlier editions restored.

These complete journals show that Scott recognized early on that his preparations for the expedition were insufficient, that he blamed his colleagues for his own shortcomings, and that, after having discovered that Amundsen had reached the Pole before him, he clung to the hope that he could get home fast and "get the news through first." Also included (and translated for the first time into English) are the journals of Amundsen and his team companion Olav Bjaaland, which run parallel to Scott's and highlight the relative pace and position of the two expeditions on a daily basis.

On a day when the Norwegian team covered fifteen miles in six and a half hours (Amundsen cheerfully describing it as "our best day up here"), Scott's team was exhausted from having man-hauled for eleven hours, covering just four miles (Scott describing it as "a most damnably dismal day"). On another day, a blizzard forced the British team to shelter in their tent, whereas the Norwegians pushed on. The comparisons between the two team leaders reveal that one was a professional explorer and the other a gutsy but misguided amateur.

After Huntford's exhaustive review of the expedition's evidence, some would say that the Scott myth has been more or less laid to rest, but controversy around it rages on. Scott's elevation to heroic status probably says more about the British psyche than anything else: his popularity soared after the World War I, when the country yearned for a hero around whom they could unite. Had he lived he probably would have been forgotten. Instead, his failure and subsequent death bestowed upon him a kind of untouchable nobility and the British, according to Huntford, "have a perverse attraction to romantic heroes who fail rather than to Homeric ones who succeed." The backlash against Scott simply reflected a cultural shift in Britain when the heroism he represented — a kind of mindless gallantry — was no longer held in such high regard.

REALITY CHECK
A HEAVY LOAD

When Scott's sled was dug out, a geological collection weighing about forty-four pounds was discovered. Commander of the *Terra Nova* expedition ship, Edward Evans, wrote, "It seems to me extraordinary that . . . they stuck to their specimens. We dumped ours at the first big check. . . . I considered the safety of my party before the value of the records . . . apparently Scott did not."

French Revolutionary doctor Joseph Guillotin invented the guillotine.

The "humane" decapitation machine known as the guillotine has long been associated with the bloody events of the French Revolution. Adopted by the French National Assembly in 1791, the guillotine became the main official method of execution during the revolution's Reign of Terror (September 1793 to July 1794), beheading the likes of King Louis XVI, Marie Antoinette, and Maximilien Robespierre, along with thousands of French citizens. It's commonly assumed that the guillotine's namesake, Doctor Joseph-Ignace Guillotin, a French physician and secretary to the National Constituent Assembly in France, invented it.

However, the guillotine — or at least similar decapitation machines — actually predates the French Revolution by several centuries. Records dating back to around 1286 show that a similar device known as the

Halifax Gibbet was used for executions in the market-place of Halifax in West Yorkshire, England. A machine similar to the French guillotine can also be seen in a sixteenth-century engraving entitled *The Execution of Murcod Ballagh near to Merton in Ireland 1307*, and then there is the Scottish Maiden, a machine modeled after the Halifax Gibbet that was used for execution from the mid-sixteenth century onward. In Italy, there was the *Mannaia*, and a mechanism known as a *Fallbeil* (falling axe) was also used in various German states from the seventeenth century onward.

REALITY CHECK

A POPULAR METHOD OF EXECUTION

The guillotine remained the official method of execution in France until the death penalty was abolished there in 1981. The last guillotining occurred in 1977, the last public execution (outside what is now the Palais de Justice, near Versailles) in 1939. The guillotine was also adopted as an official method of execution by both the German Empire and the subsequent Weimar Republic. Adolf Hitler utilized the mechanism, and between 1933 and 1945 about 16,500 people were executed by guillotine in Germany and Austria.

Dr. Joseph Guillotin, therefore, did not invent the device, he simply proposed to the French Legislative Assembly in 1789 that this fairly common method of decapitation should become the sole method of execution in France. Opposition to traditional forms of execution—such as hanging, burning, and beheading by sword or axe (usually reserved only for the rich and powerful)—had been growing in France, due mainly to the philosophies of the Enlightenment, which argued for a more humanitarian approach to execution, irrespective of the rank or status of the guilty party.

Dr. Guillotin's description of the machine—"This mechanism falls like thunder; the head flies off, blood spurts, the man is no more"—was, according to some accounts, met with nervous laughter, and was at first rejected by the Assembly. It wasn't until 1791 that the Assembly agreed to its use, having been convinced of its effectiveness in causing an instant and humane death, decreeing that "every person condemned to the death penalty shall have his head severed."

By this point the initiative had passed from Dr. Guillotin to Dr. Antoine Louis, the secretary of the Academy of Surgeons. A German harpsichord-maker and engineer, Tobias Schmidt, built the first prototype and tested it on animals—as well as on some stocky

*(L) The Halifax Gibbet and (R) Schmidt's
guillotine with its beveled-edged triangular blade*

human corpses from the Bicêtre hospital outside of
Paris. The Assembly approved Schmidt's revised model,
which changed the curved blade of the original device
to a beveled-edged triangular blade. The first execution
took place on April 25, 1792, when convicted criminal
Nicolas Pelletier was beheaded in the Place de Grève.

Copies of Schmidt's guillotine were sent out beyond
Paris to all of France's new *départements*, and there
was to be no local variation. Originally known as the

louison or *louisette*, after Dr. Antoine Louis, the name gradually evolved into the more familiar *guillotine*. The macabre image of the device transfixed Europe, spawning a host of nicknames, such as "Madame Guillotine" and "the national razor."

During the Terror, thousands were sent to the guillotine. By 1795, more than 1,000 people in Paris alone had been beheaded, and by the end of the Revolution in 1799, some 16,000 people across France had been killed by decapitation. And yet, of the estimated 30,000 who died during the Terror, the vast majority were killed by other means. Many were shot, drowned, or beaten to death by mobs, as in Lyon between December 4 and 8, 1793, when hundreds of dissidents were lined up in front of open graves and shot by cannon.

REALITY CHECK
WITHOUT DISCRIMINATION

It's commonly believed that the vast majority of the guillotine's victims were members of the aristocracy. In fact, 85 percent of those killed by the guillotine were commoners, with some 1,200 members of the nobility beheaded by the device.

Despite this, the guillotine became the preeminent symbol of the revolution's terror—the swift and brutal dispenser of justice. Although new to France, it wasn't in itself a new invention, but a refinement of a device that had been in operation for hundreds of years before Dr. Guillotin was even born.

MINI MYTH

DR. GUILLOTIN

Other myths report that Dr. Guillotin was himself beheaded by the machine that bears his name. Although briefly imprisoned toward the end of the Reign of Terror, he was released in 1794 after Robespierre fell from power and lived to the ripe old age of seventy-six. His family petitioned the French government to rename the guillotine, in a bid to dissociate themselves from the butchery of the Terror. When the government refused, the Guillotin family changed their surname.

The Man in the Iron Mask was Louis XIV's brother.

"**M**an in the Iron Mask" was the name given to a French prisoner who was held in custody between 1669 and 1703 during the reign of King Louis XIV (1643–1715). Imprisoned in various French jails, it was said that his face was always covered either by a black velvet cloth or an iron mask, and that he was guarded by two men ready to kill him should he remove his disguise. The identity of the enigmatic figure was never revealed and has been the focus of fierce debate (and romantic speculation) ever since.

The legend of the masked prisoner has spawned countless films and novels, most famously the third installment of Alexandre Dumas's 1850 saga *The Three Musketeers*. And yet, while the story of the Man in the Iron Mask might seem like pure fabrication, documentary evidence—correspondence between prison and government officials—shows that the tale has some truth.

He's been very quiet these past few days.
I think his jaw hinge has rusted up again!

The mysterious prisoner, originally named by authorities as Eustache Dauger, was first imprisoned in 1669 at the fortress of Pignerol in Piedmont under the governorship of Bénigne Dauvergne de Saint-Mars. Louis XIV's war minister, the Marquis de Louvois, had previously written to Saint-Mars informing him of the imminent arrival of the prisoner, who should be securely guarded and threatened with death should he speak of anything other than his most immediate needs. The letter and the circumstances surrounding his captivity suggest that this man was no ordinary prisoner but someone who obviously possessed information that posed a real threat to the security of the realm or to Louvois himself.

Saint-Mars subsequently took Dauger to two other French prisons and finally in 1698 to the Bastille in Paris, where an officer of the prison, Lieutenant Etienne du Junca, wrote that Saint-Mars "brought with him, in a litter, a longtime prisoner, whom he had in custody in Pignerol, and whom he kept always masked, and whose name has not been given to me, nor recorded." In 1703 the prisoner reportedly died and was buried under the name of "Marchioly." Du Junca noted his death, referring to the deceased as "the unknown prisoner who has worn a black velvet mask since his arrival in 1698." Du Junca never referred to an iron mask, nor does any other reliable contemporary source mention one.

It was the writer and philosopher Voltaire who first claimed that the prisoner wore an iron mask—"a movable, hinged lower jaw held in place by springs"—in his *Questions sur L'Encyclopédie*, published some time between 1770 and 1772. In this first historical account of the Man in the Iron Mask, Voltaire (among others) also claimed that the prisoner was the illegitimate older brother (son of Queen Anne of Austria but not of Louis XIII) of Louis XIV which would have complicated the line of succession.

A prisoner of royal descent could have explained the extraordinary circumstances surrounding his captivity, which included the need to conceal his identity and the reverence with which his jailers apparently treated him. This theory, however, presumes that Cardinal Mazarin (Chief Minister of France) had fathered a child with Queen Anne, and, while the two were close, there's no evidence to suggest any sexual impropriety between them.

MINI MYTH
THE MYTH CONTINUED . . .

Among other more fanciful suggestions, it was rumored (admittedly about a century after the Man in the Iron Mask's imprisonment) that the prisoner was the king's older brother and had fathered a child during his incarceration. The child had been sent to Corsica to be taken in by the Bonaparte family, which conveniently made Napoleon Bonaparte a direct descendent of the king. It is an appealing and fanciful notion, but no evidence exists to suggest it could actually be true.

The brother theory proved popular with Dumas and various Hollywood filmmakers (including the 1998 Leonardo DiCaprio film *The Man in the Iron Mask*) who proposed that the prisoner was the identical twin brother of Louis XIV, whose birth had been hidden. According to this theory, he was raised secretly away from court, returned years later to claim his inheritance, and was then imprisoned. A mask would have seemed a sensible precaution for a prisoner who bore a striking resemblance to the king. And yet no documentary evidence supports this theory, and one can presume it would have been impossible for the queen to conceal the birth and upbringing of a "secret" twin brother.

As speculation to the identity of the masked prisoner has broadened, among the more convincing cases have identified the Man in the Iron Mask as prisoners Charles de Batz d'Artagnan, Antonio Ercole Matthioli, or Eustace Dauger. D'Artagnan was the famously indiscreet womanizer and captain of the First Company of Musketeers, who was imprisoned in the Bastille following a quarrel with Louis XIV's minister, Louvois. The theory goes that d'Artagnan was in possession of embarrassing secrets about the king's close associates and that Louvois privately arranged for him to be imprisoned without the king's knowledge.

Prison documentation shows that the other candidates, Matthioli and Dauger, were the only two prisoners at Pignerol who could have been brought to the Bastille in 1698. Matthioli (whose name resembles the prisoner's burial name of Marchioly) was an Italian diplomat who negotiated between the Louis XIV and the Duke of Mantua in the selling of Casale Monferrato. During negotiations, Matthioli double-crossed everyone involved and was eventually seized by the French and thrown into Pignerol in 1679. However, because everyone knew about Matthioli's crimes, there would have been no need to keep his identity secret. Also, others claim that Matthioli died in 1681, not 1703.

The more likely candidate was the valet Eustace Dauger, whose master was Roux de Marsilly (Marchioly may be a misspelling of Marsilly?), a Huguenot who had tried to stir up a Protestant alliance against Louis XIV for which he was publicly tortured to death in Paris in 1669. Others have suggested that Dauger was a valet named "Danger" or "D'angers" who had botched a political assassination on behalf of the French secretary of state, however no theory has proved conclusive.

Despite the many colorful, convincing (and not

MINI MYTH

THE SKELETON IN THE CLOSET

The myth of the iron mask took on symbolic importance during the upheavals of the French Revolution. The masked prisoner, incarcerated for unknown reasons for thirty years, symbolized the tyranny of an increasingly unpopular monarchy. When the Bastille was stormed in 1789, rumors circulated (and rumor it remained) that a skeleton was found hidden in the bowels of the prison, chained to a wall with an iron mask on its skull.

so convincing) theories put forward, there is still no definitive answer to the Man in the Iron Mask's true identity, though it's safe to say the idea he was Louis XIV's brother—and that the mask was iron—are without much foundation. The secrecy surrounding the unknown prisoner has bred a huge amount of speculation and romantic fancy, creating a myth far more spectacular than the reality. It's a legend that has continued to grip the public imagination, a story riddled with mystery that has in the process generated some of the very worst—but nonetheless entertaining— examples of how they got it wrong.

Australia was established purely as a penal colony, a dumping ground for Britain's convicts.

In 1788 a fleet of British ships arrived on the eastern shores of Australia. After checking out Botany Bay, where Lieutenant James Cook had landed eighteen years earlier, the fleet moved on to Port Jackson, where they established a settlement at Sydney Cove on January 26, 1788. The fleet of eleven ships carried around 1,000 settlers, 751 of whom were British convicts sentenced to "transportation"—banishment to a land halfway across the world.

Over the next eighty years around 160,000 convicts were transported to the new Australian colonies of New South Wales, Van Diemen's Land (Tasmania), and Western Australia. The traditional view is that Australia was originally established by the British government purely as a kind of dumping ground for British convicts, as corroborated by historian Norman Bartlett in 1976: "There is no evidence that either Prime Minister Pitt or any member of this cabinet thought of Botany Bay as anything more than a convenient place distant enough for the safe disposal of social waste." It was a colonial experiment that had never been tried before, nor has it since then been repeated.

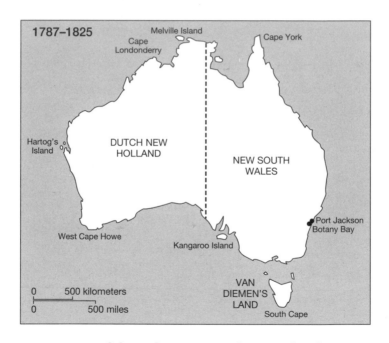

A map of the colonization of Australia during the early stages of transportation

Yet others have challenged this assumption (including Geoffrey Blainey in *The Tyranny of Distance*), partly because there appears to be no logical sense in building a prison 12,000 miles away, unless there were deeper motives behind the decision. The discovery of new artifacts has shed light on what these motives might have been. "A Proposal for Establishing a Settlement in New South Wales" is one such document, which was submitted to the government in 1783 by the American Loyalist James Matra, who had been aboard Cook's historic voyage to Botany Bay in 1770. Matra's justifications for settlement included: good soil suitable for sugar, cotton, and tobacco plantation; the potential for whaling, flax cultivation, and the availability of naval timber for the home market; and its usefulness as a trading base with China, Korea, and Japan. Matra also proposed that the colony be settled by "Americans who had remained loyal to Britain in the War of Independence" (such as himself), but this idea was ultimately rejected.

It was only in 1784, following a meeting with Lord Sydney, Home Secretary, that the proposal was amended to include "transportees [convicts] among the settlers as cultivators in their own right rather than as forced labor." Since convicts could no longer be sent to America (following the Revolutionary War), the British government had been considering transporting convicts to West Africa (a much shorter and cheaper journey), but was ultimately swayed by Matra's more comprehensive proposal.

REALITY CHECK
TRANSPORTATION

Transportation was an integral part of the English and Irish systems of punishment, and up until the Revolutionary War in America, around 1,000 criminals a year were sent to either Virginia or Maryland. British jails and hulks (makeshift floating prisons) were full to bursting with rising numbers of criminals (due to an increased population), and transportation helped to relieve the pressure put on the British prisons.

A wide range of fairly minor offenses could result in transportation, and a number of the convicts sent in the early transports to Australia had only seven-year sentences. (Many of the women—who made up twenty percent of the first convict settlers—were first-time offenders.) Had the government intended the colony of Australia to be nothing other than a gulag, one would assume that they would have sent only the very worst convicts. Instead, a great majority of convicts were working men and women with a range of skills, whose seven-year sentences would provide enough time in which to set up the infrastructure of the colony. On later ships, convicts were also made up of political and social nonconformists, along with a smattering of wayward young men from the gentry and bourgeoisie classes. (Charles Dickens sent two of his less academically gifted sons to Australia.)

It is assumed that convicts bound for Australia suffered appalling conditions (as deaths on board wouldn't have mattered to the authorities if they were simply seen as "social waste"). Yet there is evidence to show that efforts were made to ensure the convicts arrived in relatively good health. Ships were inspected for seaworthiness, which Philip Knightley notes, in *Australia: Biography of a Nation,* made "the convict voyage to Australia . . . distinctly safer than emigrant voyages either to Australia or to America."

Before transportation, many of the inmates were stripped of their vermin-infested clothes, bathed, and held for four days while being inspected by surgeons for infection, and many of the ships carried a surgeon-general whose main aim was to limit the number of deaths en route. Later ships, particularly those administered by private contractors, suffered higher death rates, although some of those deaths could have been borne from diseases previously contracted by prisoners. While life on board the ships could indeed be brutal—prisoners were generally kept below deck in chains or behind bars—many of the convicts were provided with one substantial meal a day, religious instruction, and even a daily dose of lemon juice to avoid scurvy.

Once the first convicts arrived at Botany Bay, they were not simply worked to death in a gulag-like prison, but were integrated into a system of labor in which all people, whatever their crime, were employed. Convicts formed the majority of the colony's population in the first few decades, although the first free settlers (who were given free passage, land, and provisions) also began arriving in 1793. Convicts were allocated work to suit their skills, and the unskilled were often involved in manual labor, such as road-building.

Conditions could be harsh, and discipline was strictly enforced with flogging, leg irons, or transportation to stricter penal colonies set up at Norfolk Island or Port Arthur. From 1801, some convicts were rewarded with Tickets of Leave that gave them certain freedoms, and by the 1820s few convicts served their full sentences. By the mid-1830s, only around six percent of the convict population was "locked up," the majority working for free settlers and various other authorities. Transportation finally ended in 1868, when the population in Australia stood at a very healthy one million and the colonies were able to support themselves and grow without the need for convicts.

Although the transport of convicts to Australia did

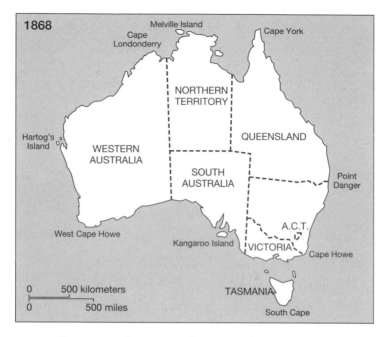

This map shows just how much Australia had changed toward the end of transportation.

relieve the pressure put upon the prison authorities of Britain, the new colony was not viewed purely as a simple dumping ground for unwanted criminals. Australia's abundant resources, strategic position, and proximity to the Far East were also motivating factors, while the convicts provided a cheap labor force who could set up the infrastructure of the colony. Conditions for many of the transported convicts were brutal, but the establishment of Australia actually proved to be one of the more humane prison experiences of the eighteenth century and a social experiment (at least for the white settlers) that resulted in a resounding success.

REALITY CHECK
NAVAL BASE POTENTIAL

The decision to colonize New South Wales was also set against the backdrop of potential war against France, Holland, and Spain. Matra showed how the colony would provide a useful naval base for attacks on Dutch possessions in the East Indies and Spanish colonies in South America and the Philippines. Over the next few decades, whenever war with Spain seemed a possibility, plans were revived to make New South Wales Britain's main naval base in the region.

President Roosevelt's New Deal saved capitalism and lifted the United States out of the Depression.

It's traditionally thought that after President Hoover did nothing to tackle the Great Depression in America, President Franklin D. Roosevelt confronted it head on, with a dazzling series of economic reforms known as the New Deal. This program, passed by Congress between 1933 and 1936, rescued American capitalism and ultimately led to greater prosperity and renewed confidence in the economy. Roosevelt was hailed as the great savior of capitalism and democracy, and a man who had restored belief and hope in America.

As Roosevelt took office in 1933, he promised a "New Deal" for the American people in the first one hundred days of his administration—a program that would provide relief for the unemployed and poor, recover the nation's economy, and reform the financial system. In a bid to stabilize the banking industry, Roosevelt closed all the banks until Congress passed the Emergency Banking Act (an act that had actually been carefully crafted by Treasury officials during Hoover's presidency). Sound banks could then open under Treasury supervision and with federal loans if needed. In June of 1933 the Federal Deposit Insurance Corporation (FDIC) was set up, which insured bank deposits of up to $2,500 and then $5,000.

To deal with deflation, the U.S. currency was taken off the gold standard (except for foreign exchange) in the early spring of 1934. Other early reforms that formed part of Roosevelt's "First New Deal" included: forcing businesses to set prices with the government and instituting regulations to prevent aggressive competition through the NRA (National Recovery Administration); setting minimum prices and wages; cutting agricultural production to raise prices through the Agricultural Adjustment Act. By 1935, the "Second New Deal" added social security, a jobs program for the unemployed, and stimulus for the growth of trade unions through the National Labor Relations Board.

The economy temporarily improved, and by 1937 industrial production exceeded pre-Depression levels of 1929, although unemployment remained at eleven percent. In autumn of 1937 the economy took another sharp downturn, and unemployment levels reached nineteen percent. The Depression lingered on, only lifting in 1941 when America joined World War II. Historian Doris Kearns Goodwin wrote, "The America over which Roosevelt presided in 1940 was in its eleventh year of depression. No decline in American history has been so deep, so lasting, so far reaching."

Roosevelt's New Deal program of "relief, recovery, and reform" ultimately failed, and, according to some economists, actually caused the depression to persist longer than it otherwise would have done. In a 2004 article for the *Journal of Political Economy*, economists Harold L. Cole and Lee E. Ohanian maintain that Roosevelt's policies prolonged the downturn by as many as seven years.

Central to Cole and Ohanian's argument was the damaging effect of the NRA: its control of wages and prices effectively created industry-wide cartels that restricted production and raised prices, which in turn distorted normal market conditions and prevented recovery. Roosevelt himself recognized this: "The American economy has become a concealed cartel system [. . .] The disappearance of price competition is one of the primary causes of the present difficulties."

REALITY CHECK

HOOVER'S FOUNDATIONS

Herbert Hoover's presidency (1929–33) coincided with the Wall Street Crash of 1929 and the ensuing Great Depression of the 1930s. Like his presidential predecessors during earlier depressions, Hoover's first instinct was to do nothing, with the hope that the "natural processes" of the economy would lead to an upturn. As the economy worsened, however, Hoover took firm action. At first he attempted to extract voluntary pledges from businesses to maintain production and employment levels, while encouraging state and municipal governments to increase public works spending. When this failed, he turned to more direct federal intervention by increasing government spending on public works (the Hoover Dam and other construction projects cost the government some $50 million), buying up surplus farm produce through the Farm Board, and endorsing legislation to establish the Reconstruction Finance Corporation (RFC). The RFC—whose purpose was to lend federal money to railroads, farmers, and financial institutions—would eventually become a key agency of Roosevelt's New Deal. Although Hoover ultimately failed to reverse the depression (or provide relief for the poor), his presidential term initiated and provided the testing ground for a more direct federal intervention.

Cole and Ohanian similarly argued that the Agricultural Adjustment Act worsened the situation by using tax revenue to pay farmers to restrict production. Not only did this put more pressure on the taxpayer, but it also led to a rise in food prices and substantial unemployment among farmworkers (affecting as many as 2 million people). Although Roosevelt's first one hundred days and intermittent radio broadcasts (known as "fireside chats") served to soothe the nation and boost public confidence, Roosevelt's critics claim that his administration led to a great deal of uncertainty and apprehension among American businessmen, discouraging much-needed long-term investment.

Additionally, Roosevelt's massive funding of government-initiated projects certainly created jobs within the public sector, but economists John Joseph Wallis and Daniel K. Benjamin argue that revenues raised for these public ventures diverted capital and jobs from the private sector. These underlying and far less evident causes actually hampered the recovery of the private sector, added to long-term unemployment levels, and had disastrous consequences for the economy.

On the surface, Roosevelt's reforms were impressive: he provided much-needed relief for the poor and those who could not help themselves; he constructed

thousands of roads, schools, and other public buildings; and he "connected" with the American people
with his brave series of interventionist measures. And
yet many of the reforms of the New Deal served only
to distort normal market conditions and prevent recovery of the private sector. Roosevelt was no savior
of capitalism; some of his reforms actually shack-
led the natural forces of the free market system and
thereby hindered the country's ability to pull itself out
of depression.

Abraham Lincoln's main aim in fighting the Civil War was to free the slaves.

Abraham Lincoln is regarded as one of America's greatest presidents. He successfully led his country through the Civil War of 1861 to 1865, preserved the Union, and abolished slavery throughout the United States. It's commonly assumed that the issue of slave emancipation spurred Lincoln—to invade the southern states. It's an impressive theory, and worthy of such a fine president, but not quite true.

It took four years for the Union forces of the North to crush the Confederates of the South, and in that time Lincoln's objectives changed. At the outset of hostilities, Lincoln had two basic aims: to preserve the Union and to halt further expansion of slavery into the

REALITY CHECK

LINCOLN'S STANCE
AT THE OUTSET OF WAR

Abraham Lincoln declared this in a 1858 public debate on the future of slavery:

> I am not, nor ever have been in favor of bringing about in any way the social and political equality of the white and black races, that I am not nor ever have been in favor of making voters or jurors of negroes, nor of qualifying them to hold office, nor to intermarry with white people. . . . I do not perceive that because the white man is to have the superior position the negro should be denied everything. I do not understand that because I do not want a negro woman for a slave I must necessarily want her for a wife. My understanding is that I can just let her alone.

West. But as the war continued the abolition of slavery became his new and primary motive.

Although the slave-owning states of the South were convinced that Lincoln and his victorious Republican Party were hell-bent on emancipating their slaves,

Lincoln at the outset of war was no abolitionist. At the end of his inaugural speech in March of 1861, he stressed this specific point in an attempt to pacify the Southern secessionists: "I have no purpose, directly or indirectly, to interfere with the institution of slavery in

REALITY CHECK
Southern Secession

After Lincoln became president in 1860, seven slave-owning states in the South seceded from the Union and formed the Confederate States of America (also known as the Confederacy), electing Jefferson Davis as their president. With the North growing in wealth and population, the secessionists feared that Lincoln and his victorious Republican Party would extend the abolition of slavery across the United States. Hostilities began in 1861 when Confederate troops fired on Union forces at Fort Sumter in South Carolina (one of only two federal properties in the South to remain in Union hands and which Lincoln, although averse to war, refused to surrender). Four more slave states joined the South's fight for independence, and war was declared between the Union forces (which included twenty mostly northern free states and five border slave states) and the Confederate army.

the States where it exists [. . .] We are not enemies but friends. We must not be enemies." His words proved futile, however, as by April 12, Confederate and Union troops were locked in battle at Fort Sumter, South Carolina, and within weeks another four Southern states had joined the Confederacy. Prior to becoming president, Lincoln had frequently spoken about his moral objections to slavery, although he often modified his stance according to the audience he was addressing. To some, he railed against the evil institution of slavery; to others he stressed the superiority of white over black. (And in his home state of Illinois he never contested the inequality of blacks who could neither vote nor testify in court against whites.)

Lincoln's views on slavery came to the fore in 1858 when he engaged with Stephen A. Douglas, senior Senator for Illinois, in a series of highly publicized debates on the future of slavery in the United States. Douglas supported the view of "popular sovereignty," that settlers in new territories should have the right to choose slavery. He tried to wreck Lincoln's chances of election by painting him as an out-and-out abolitionist. Lincoln adopted the Republican stance—slavery should be outlawed in the new territories to prevent its further spread. However, he made it clear that he had no intention to

REALITY CHECK

PRESERVATION OF THE UNION

In September 1862, Lincoln wrote a public letter to *Harper's Weekly* in which he said:

> If I could save the Union without freeing any slave I would do it, and if I could save the Union by freeing all the slaves I would do it. And if I could save it by freeing some and leaving others alone, I would also do that.

abolish slavery in the states where it already existed, nor was he a champion of racial equality. Still, at this stage Lincoln's key aim was to preserve the Union.

Eight months into the Civil War, Lincoln still looked to appease the Southern states and was adamant that the suppression of hostilities "shall not degenerate into a violent and remorseless revolutionary struggle." He even suggested to Congress that any slaves freed as result of the struggle be resettled abroad. Yet the war raged on, and events soon slipped out of Lincoln's control. With so many Southern men fighting, the slave system they left behind began to disintegrate as slaves fled to Union lines.

The untapped resources of escaped slaves proved more appealing to Lincoln, and in July 1862 Congress passed legislation to allow the enlistment of black soldiers within the army. Reconciliation with the South no longer seemed possible, and more and more Northerners aligned themselves with the abolitionists. Still, Lincoln publicly maintained that his only goal was to save the Union, and that the pursuit of war was entirely divorced from the issue of slavery.

In September 1862, Lincoln signed the Emancipation Proclamation, which declared that all slaves of the Confederate States that did not return to the Union by January 1, 1863, would be freed—3.1 million out of America's 4 million slaves would be liberated. (The bill excluded roughly 800,000 slaves from the border states that had not seceded from the Union.) Despite Lincoln's earlier intentions, the war had evolved into a revolutionary struggle in which slavery had become a key issue. Lincoln still maintained that his main goal was preservation of the Union, but he also recognized that this could now only be achieved through emancipation. In 1863, he wrote in a letter: "The use of the colored troops constitute the heaviest blow yet dealt to the Rebellion, and that at least one of these important successes could not have been achieved when it was but for the aid of black soldiers."

By the time Lincoln delivered his famous Gettysburg Address in November of 1863, his public justification for war had shifted. Invoking the principles of the Declaration of Independence, which infamously declares that all men are created equal, he now defined the Civil War as a struggle not merely for the Union but also as a new birth of freedom that would bring true equality to all of its citizens. After the passing of the Emancipation Proclamation, Lincoln lobbied Congress for a constitutional amendment outlawing slavery throughout America—this was finally passed on January 31, 1865.

Lincoln summarized the events of the war in a letter to Albert G. Hodges in 1864:

> I claim not to have controlled events, but confess plainly that events have controlled me. Now, at the end of three years' struggle the nation's condition is not what either party, or any man devised, or expected.

MINI MYTH

THE GETTYSBURG MYTH

In November 1863, Lincoln was invited to speak at a funeral service for the fallen soldiers of the Battle of Gettysburg, fought four months earlier. Posterity tells us that he scribbled his famous three-minute speech of ten sentences (now one of the most quoted speeches in history) on the back of an envelope en route to the service. This is, in truth, a myth, as Lincoln wrote the draft of his speech back in Washington and, according to David J. Eicher in *Gettysburg Battlefield*, took with him to the service five copies of the speech, none of which were written on the back of an envelope. The myth probably took hold because Lincoln's short and now legendary speech followed the two-hour (and now forgotten) speech of Massachusetts orator Edward Everett.

The United States entered World War I at the last minute and contributed little to the Allied victory.

I t was (and still is) a commonly held belief that the United States contributed little to the eventual victory of the Allies. America failed to offer practical help on the Western Front and entered only to have influence over peace terms. But the reality is that America played a crucial role in the Allied war effort both before and after she sent troops to France.

At the outbreak of hostilities in 1914, President Woodrow Wilson stood firm by America's customary policy of isolation from the political affairs of Europe. America's melting-pot population of European peoples, of whom 8 million had been born in Germany, also added weight to the argument. While critics joked that Wilson was too timid to fight (shells that failed to explode were nicknamed "Wilsons" by soldiers), the president believed that the United States had a unique moral role to play, which, he maintained, would rise above the conflict and shape its eventual peace.

REALITY CHECK
AMERICAN IMPORTS

Britain relied heavily on America for artillery, ammunition, aircraft, and motor vehicles, and by 1916, thirty percent of British food was being imported from America. As the war progressed, U.S. banks made massive loans to the Allied forces, lending, by the end of the war, $10 billion to the Allies while the British blockaded much needed imports from getting into Germany. These huge loans, imports of vital goods, and the "unwritten sympathy" of the United States for the plight of Britain and her allies was of critical importance in the defeat of the Central Powers. As Gordon Corrigan maintains in his book *Mud, Blood and Poppycock*:

> American industry and American governmental tolerance were essential to the British war effort long before the United States entered the war, and while Britain might still have won the war without them, it would have taken far longer and would have taken many more lives.

Neutrality also gave a real boost to the economy of America, which in 1914 had been on the brink of recession. New markets opened up around the world, and increased demand from the warring nations boosted production and profit in the United States. In practice, however, the Allies, and not the Central Powers, benefited mostly from America's increased industrial and agricultural output, thanks largely to its vast federal reserves and to Great Britain's tightly controlled naval blockade of Germany.

During the years 1914 to 1916, U.S. exports to Great Britain and France multiplied from a value of $750 million to $2.75 billion; whereas, exports to Germany—which had fewer financial reserves than Britain and was concentrating on military expenditure—slumped from $345 million to a mere $2 million. The subsequent German shortage of vital raw materials is considered by some to have been a major contributory factor to the eventual Allied victory.

Early in 1917, the United States was finally provoked to consider military action following the publication of the Zimmermann Telegram (which revealed the threat of a German/Mexican alliance) combined with all-out submarine warfare by German U-boats against vessels of all kind, including neutral American ones. On

It says here the war was
already won before we got here.

April 6, 1917, the United States declared war on Germany, although Wilson reasserted that the agenda of the United States was different from that of the Allies: "We have no selfish ends to serve. We desire no conquest, nor dominion." Wilson saw himself as having the moral upper hand, and he also clearly sought to influence, if not dictate, eventual peace terms. In July 1917, he maintained that "England and France have not the same views with regard to the peace that we have by any means. When the war is over we can force them to our way of thinking, because by that time they will, among other things, be financially in our hands."

Committed to war, the United States rapidly set about preparing its fairly feeble military (ranked seventeenth in the world, alongside Argentina) for combat. Its army required enormous expansion, which was achieved through the conscription of some 2.8 million men, while 24 million men were registered for the draft. The training of conscripts delayed matters, as did the acute shortage of ships to take them across the Atlantic. By the end of 1917, however, around 200,000 American soldiers had been transported to Europe, and by October 1918 around 1,800,000 U.S. men were fighting on the Western Front.

The American Expeditionary Forces (the term for U.S. soldiers who participated in the conflict) saw their first major action on May 28, 1918, when American soldiers—known as "doughboys"—held the front line at Cantigny (with the help of French artillery) and eventually captured it from the Germans. In June, U.S. forces drove the Germans out of Château-Thierry, and in July and August, nine U.S. divisions helped with the Aisne-Marne counteroffensive, recapturing the Allied line between Reims and Soissons. At the end of September, more than 1 million U.S. soldiers (now formed into the First U.S. Army) drove into the Argonne Forest toward the Hindenburg Line, but their inexperience and poor strategy brought heavy casualties, with 120,000 either dead or wounded.

By the end of October, the British Third and Fourth Armies were over the River Selle, and all along the lines, the Allied and American forces were advancing, while the Germans retreated. Morale among the German forces plummeted as defeat approached, and they were plagued with mutiny and desertion. The Allied forces, on the other hand, attacked with what Gordon Corrigan in *Mud, Blood and Poppycock* describes as "a seemingly inexhaustible supply of American manpower."

The massive autumn offensive, combined with the economic blockade of Germany, resulted in an abrupt end to hostilities, with the armistice coming into effect on November 11, 1918. Had the war continued beyond 1918, the American military was poised to grow bigger than the combined forces of the British and French, and it was this knowledge that prompted

General Ludendorff to launch the German offensive in the spring of 1918, a decision that cost him the war.

While U.S. casualties (more than 100,000 deaths) were relatively low compared to those of the other Entente forces, they occurred in a short span of time

A map of the Western Front, 1918

and were keenly felt by the American nation, who had never before sent a mass army to a foreign war. The contribution of the Americans in the outcome of the World War I was critical. Had they not supplied vital supplies, financial loans, and, finally, their men, the war could have continued for several more grueling years and may even have swung against an Allied victory.

WRONG

The Great Famine in China was the unintentional consequence of Chairman Mao's economic reforms.

During the years 1958 to 1961, the People's Republic of China underwent a series of economic and social reforms known as the Great Leap Forward. The Communist regime of Mao Zedong aimed to transform China into a modern Communist society with an economy and industrial output that would surpass that of the Soviet Union and Great Britain within fifteen years. Yet its program of agricultural and industrial reforms, which included the prohibition of private farming and radical collectivization, led to catastrophe and the loss of millions of lives from starvation and deprivation. The idea that this loss of lives was an unintentional consequence of the Great Leap Forward disregards the Maoist regime's deliberate role in exacerbating the ensuing catastrophe.

Original estimates for "excess deaths" during the Great Leap Forward ranged from 15 million to 32 million, yet the recent opening up of thousands of central and provincial documents, including secret party committee reports and public security documents, have revealed that these figures are woefully inadequate. This recent evidence suggests that at least 45 million people may have lost their lives prematurely during the years 1958 to 1962.

Frank Dikötter's book *Mao's Great Famine* draws from these new archival documents and describes how its victims were deliberately deprived of food and basic needs, and worked to death or killed as a result of the systematic violence and terror. Dikötter argues that the word "famine" fails to encompass the many ways people died, since it implies that the deaths were simply "the unintended consequence" of the state's economic reforms. Instead, there was a large element of deliberate mass killing, and of systematic neglect of the type usually associated with Stalin, Hitler, or Pol Pot, and one of the worst examples of mass murder in Chinese and world history.

Signs of famine first appeared in China in 1958; by the following year it was widespread. The new archive material shows that decisions made by the government's top officials led directly to severe food shortages and famine. Many of the regime's officials knew that people were starving to death, but those close to Mao indulged his visionary whims while others exaggerated the effectiveness of his reforms. Mao himself was aware of the famine, and in 1959 he was quoted as saying, "When there is not enough to eat people starve to death. It is better to let half of the people die so that the other half can eat their fill."

Since 1953 farmers had been forced to sell grain to the state at prices determined by the government. However, during the years 1959 and 1962, the new data shows that Mao's government increased the grain procurement quota from its usual twenty to twenty-five percent to thirty to thirty-seven percent, at a time when the average output per head was at its lowest. Some of the grain the government procured was sold back to the farmers (at an inflated price), but much of it was exported or given as foreign aid to maintain China's reputation overseas. The needs of China's countryside were deliberately disregarded in favor of the government's "export above all else" policy.

By the end of 1958, farms and households in China's countryside were organized into some 26,000 communes. Chinese society and its economy spiraled out of control as commune workers dismantled their houses to use as fertilizer, abandoned the fields to man makeshift steel furnaces (set up to achieve Mao's frenzied steel production targets), or worked on the government's mammoth and largely useless water conservation schemes — all while their families died without food. Conditions were similarly appalling for many of China's industrial and factory workers, who were forced to meet ever increasing industrial output targets, and who also suffered from famine in large numbers. By 1961, up to half of the workforce in Beijing suffered from famine edema, the swelling caused by insufficient protein intake.

Intimidation and coercion formed the foundation of Mao's regime, and anyone who questioned his policies was declared a "rightist" and punished accordingly. Coercion of workers often escalated into extreme violence, from beatings by party officials to torture. It's now estimated that at least six to eight percent (around 2.5 million) of all the famine victims were killed or died of injuries inflicted by local officials or the militia. For the smallest offense, workers could also be sent to labor camps scattered across China or to "reeducation camps" or private gulags that were attached to most communes.

While much of the evidence is still undisclosed, it is estimated that there were around 8–9 million prisoners during each year of the Great Leap Forward, of which around 3 million people died in the labor camps during the famine. Suicide rates also grew exponentially, with between 1 and 3 million people killing themselves from 1958 to 1962. Reports also show that people resorted to a variety of desperate measures to survive, from stealing and attacking granaries to abandoning their own children.

Mao's economic reforms led not just to a shortage of food but also to a shortage of all basic essentials. Approximately thirty to forty percent of China's housing was demolished, and millions of displaced peasants were left homeless, facing winters without firewood or adequate clothing (much of China's cotton was exported abroad or fed to the textile industries). The Great Leap Forward also had a disastrous impact on the natural resources of China, with the destruction of huge swathes of forest (fifty percent of all trees in some regions), while the government's irrigation schemes reduced crop fertility on farmlands and left whole regions devastated by heavy rain and typhoons.

Although Mao's famine has been known about in the West for many decades, few Westerners are aware

REALITY CHECK
THE LONG MARCH

The Long March represents a significant episode in the history of the Communist Party of China, marking the ascent to power of Mao Zedong as its leader. Official accounts tell us that between October 1934 and October 1935 the Central Red Army, under the guidance of Mao, fought its way north from Yudu in the Jiangzi province to Yan'an in the province of Shaanxi in a bid to escape from the Kuomintang (Chinese Nationalist Party). The over 80,000-strong army took 370 days to cover some 8,000 miles (12,500 kilometers) over very difficult terrain. The Long March came to seal the personal prestige of Mao, who oversaw the defeat of the Nationalist forces and its leader Chiang Kai-shek. However, there was not one Long March but a series of marches by various Communist armies. Mao did not control or even plan the march and was only told about it a couple of days beforehand. By the time the Red Army reached Yan'an, Mao was in full control, but he did not single-handedly defeat Chiang Kai-shek. Instead Kai-shek's own commanders had defected, kidnapped Kai-shek, and forced him to recognize the Communists so that they could all fight their common enemy: the Japanese.

of the scale or manner of the atrocities. As Professor Ilya Somin writes, "Chinese Communist atrocities are little-known even by comparison to those inflicted by Communists in Eastern Europe and the Soviet Union, possibly because the Chinese are more culturally distant from Westerners than are Eastern Europeans." The new archive material also confirms that the Chinese leadership was far from ignorant about the famine, and, as sinologist Roderick MacFarquhar writes, "[Mao] will be remembered as the ruler who initiated and presided over the worst man-made human catastrophe ever. His place in Chinese history is assured."

James Watt invented the steam engine.

Scottish-born mechanical engineer James Watt invented the steam engine, creating the driving force behind the Industrial Revolution. Well, yes and no. The man revered as one of the founding fathers of the Industrial Revolution (so much so that his name was used for the SI power unit, the "watt") *did* invent a type of steam engine that could be used in factories or mills, but he didn't invent the *first* steam engine.

Indeed, prior to Watt, quite a lot of work had already been done on the concept of the steam engine (which, in essence, uses boiling water to produce mechanical motion). Watt himself adapted a machine that had already been invented by Thomas Newcomen some seventy years earlier. Newcomen's atmospheric steam engine, first introduced in 1712, employed a piston and cylinder, and was used to pump water from deep coal mines in Britain and in Europe.

REALITY CHECK
THE HISTORY BEHIND THE ENGINE

The history of the steam engine is rich and varied. Before Newcomen, Thomas Savery had constructed and patented a similar water pump engine, the "Miner's Friend," by 1698. Newcomen himself based his engine on the experiments of Frenchman Denis Papin, who in 1679 invented a "steam digester," a device that extracted fats from bones in a high-pressured steam environment (the forerunner of the domestic pressure cooker). Even the ancient Greeks took a stab at making a steam engine, with a contraption called the "aeolipile," which consisted of a hollow globe that spun on its axis when steam pressure was applied through connecting pipes.

Watt's genius lay in the improvements he made to Newcomen's engine, so that it could be used in all sorts of industrial settings and not just for pumping water out of coal mines. Between 1763 and 1764 Watt, while working at Glasgow University, was asked to repair a model Newcomen engine. Noting that the engine design wasted energy by repeatedly heating and cooling the cylinder, Watt proposed that it use

What's his name?

That was the question!

Watt.

two cylinders, one that remained hot and one, called the condenser, that remained cold and was separated from the piston chamber. This alteration radically boosted the engine's power, improved its efficiency, and saved on coal costs. Working closely with manufacturer Matthew Boulton, Watt made further alterations to the steam engine, and by 1783 he had developed a double-acting, rotating type of engine, adding a flywheel and "governor" so that the speed of the engine could be made constant. This new type of engine could be used to power the machinery of factories and mills, and by 1800, the firm Boulton & Watt

Watt's engine

had constructed some 449 engines for use in industry.

However, contrary to popular belief, the steam engine was not immediately adopted by factories in the nineteenth century; its introduction was gradual, while many manufacturers in the first half of the century continued to rely on traditional forms of power, namely water, horse, and human power. The newer industries, however — in particular the cotton trade — made great use of the steam engine, and eventually mines, waterworks, canals, and ironworks also became reliant on steam power. Later, adaptations were made to Watt's engine so that steam power could also be used in locomotives, furnaces, and steamboats. Its use also led to the development of the machine tool industry, which allowed machines to be constructed in ever-greater complexity. The real surge in the application of steam power occurred in the latter half of the nineteenth century when it was used to drive turbines that generated electricity.

While James Watt didn't develop the *first* steam engine—that achievement lay with the primitive contraption invented by the ancient Greeks—he did play a vital role in developing a type of efficient steam engine that could be used in all manner of industrial settings. And it was this development that allowed for the engine's gradual adoption across industry during the nineteenth century.

The attack on Pearl Harbor was deliberately engineered by President Roosevelt.

On the morning of December 7, 1941, the Japanese launched a ferocious and sudden airborne attack on the U.S. Pacific Fleet stationed at Pearl Harbor on the Hawaiian island of Oahu. The Japanese succeeded in sinking or badly damaging eight U.S. battleships, three destroyers, and three cruisers, while killing or wounding 3,435 servicemen. The "date which will live in infamy," as President Franklin D. Roosevelt called it, not only sparked the Pacific War, but also ensured that America would be drawn into World War II.

With a large part of the U.S. naval strength at anchor during the attack, American forces had clearly been unprepared for the assault, and rumors almost immediately circulated as to how and why the United

States had been caught off guard. Some theorists have argued that Roosevelt provoked the Japanese into attacking in a bid to maintain his own political security while also giving him just cause to enter World War II. The argument rages on and even today, conspiracy theorists argue that American officials, from the president down, had advance knowledge of Japan's intentions but were persuaded to keep silent.

Although the attack was swift and sudden, relations between the United States and Japan had been worsening for years. Since the early 1930s, the United States had become increasingly alarmed by Japan's mounting aggression against China. War in Europe led to Japan signing the Tripartite Axis Pact with Germany and Italy in September 1940. Japan then focused its military on British, French, and Dutch colonies in Southeast Asia.

The United States continued to impose heavy embargoes on Japan, and by July 1941 trade between the two countries ceased. Three months later, the moderate government in Tokyo was taken over by the more militant General Tojo ("the Razor"), who took a hard-line approach in his negotiations with the United States. American officials responded in a similar vein, announcing that the United States would only resume trade with Japan if Japanese troops were withdrawn from China and Indochina, and if Japan supported the Nationalist government in China. With neither country backing down, negotiations ended in deadlock.

In fact, the U.S. administration knew that Japan had set a deadline for a diplomatic solution, after which, if an agreement hadn't been achieved, they would go to war. U.S. cryptanalysts had cracked Japanese diplomatic codes, and U.S. decoding machines named "Magic" enabled the Americans to read confidential Japanese messages. There were thousands of these "Magic" messages that had to be deciphered, translated, and evaluated, and, even after they were, they never revealed when or where an attack was planned. The Roosevelt administration knew that an assault was imminent, but they assumed the Japanese would strike somewhere in Southeast Asia. It never occurred to them that the Japanese would target the heavily fortified island of Oahu.

American military officials also seriously underestimated the military capabilities of Japan, and wrongly assumed that Japan was unable to mount more than one naval operation at a time. U.S. officials were totally unaware that on November 26 six Japanese aircraft carriers embarked on a flight across the western Pacific toward Pearl Harbor, because the

Japanese skillfully maintained complete radio silence and avoided sea-lanes used by merchant ships.

On December 6, "Magic" machines began decoding a fourteen-part message from Tokyo to the Japanese delegation in Washington. The final part of the message apparently instructed the Japanese delegation to break off negotiations, thus hinting at war. However, there was a delay getting the translated version of the message to the Secretary of State and Chief of the U.S. General Staff so that by the time officials received it at Pearl Harbor, the attack had already begun. For decades it was thought that this was why the United States had had no prior warning of the attack; however, academics have recently argued that this last document actually didn't amount to anything as clear-cut as a declaration of war, or a severance of diplomatic relations, as the Japanese had no intention of formally declaring war or even giving prior notice to any ending of negotiation, so even if the message had arrived before the attack, it is unclear if officials would have known what it meant.

Aside from America's inability to decipher Japan's exact motives, Roosevelt himself was in no hurry for war. He knew that the United States needed more time to build up its military capacity, and he wanted to postpone hostilities with Japan for as long as possible, as he saw the war against the Nazis in Germany as more of a priority. And even when war with Japan became increasingly likely, there is evidence to show that Roosevelt wanted to avoid appearing as the aggressor. On December 6, 1941, in answer to an adviser's question as to why the United States hadn't struck first to "prevent any sort of surprise," he responded, "No, we can't do that. We are a democracy and a peaceful people."

Since the attack, the U.S. government has made nine

REALITY CHECK
HIT AND RUN

The Pearl Harbor attack was designed to be a surprise hit-and-run raid. The Japanese planned to immobilize the U.S. fleet while they conquered crucial targets in Southeast Asia. Japan lacked natural resources, and, due to the trade embargoes by the United States, she desperately needed to secure alternative supplies. Japan also hoped that destroying the U.S. Pacific Fleet would crush American morale and cause Roosevelt to vie for peace (although it ultimately had the opposite effect in uniting the country behind war against Japan).

official inquiries (the most recent in 1995), all of which have shown that there is no foundation to the argument that Roosevelt knew about the impending attack on Pearl Harbor and deliberately failed to prevent it. Rather, the inquiries have pointed to a general underestimation of Japanese capabilities as well as impaired coordination between the army and navy, and a lack of manpower in the processing of intelligence—all of which suggest human error rather than deliberate conspiracy. Indeed, Roosevelt was privy to the same information as his officials: They were warned of imminent Japanese action, but their biggest mistake was to underestimate the military capabilities of Japan.

MINI MYTH
THE YAMAMOTO QUOTE

The Japanese Admiral Isoroku Yamamoto, who devised the attack, is famously said to have told his officers, "I fear all we have done is to awaken a sleeping giant and fill him with a terrible resolve." A memorable line—which in film adaptations makes for a dramatic scene—but, sadly, there is no record that Yamamoto actually said it.

The Italian astronomer Galileo was persecuted by the Catholic Church and imprisoned in a dark cell.

The myth holds that in the seventeenth century, the Roman Catholic Church convicted the elderly scientist Galilei Galileo (1564–1642) of heresy, whereupon he was tortured and left to rot in a dark cell. The "Galileo Affair" was perceived as a battle between scientific reason and religious superstition, an encounter that laid bare the tyranny of the Catholic Church.

However, the reality is that the charges brought against Galileo were largely motivated by fellow scientists and rivals, many of whom Galileo had insulted, bullied, and dismissed in the years preceding the publication of his *Dialogue on the Two Great World Systems* (see page 133). Galileo's enemies—and there were many— set about to discredit the astronomer and successfully convinced Pope Urban VIII (a former friend and ally of Galileo) that the *Dialogue* openly mocked the Pope's views about the universe.

In 1633 Galileo was accused of heresy and forced to stand trial. During the trial it was claimed that he had been given an injunction by Cardinal Bellarmine in 1616 to refrain from promoting or teaching the heliocentric theory (see page 133). Galileo rightly insisted that he'd never received such an injunction, only a private warning from Bellarmine not to "hold" or "defend" the view that the earth moved. In Galileo's view, the *Dialogue* did not conflict with Bellarmine's warning as it presented both sides of the argument. The court eventually agreed not to press the most serious charge of "violation of an injunction" as long as Galileo pleaded guilty to the charge that the *Dialogue* gave the impression that he was defending the heliocentric theory (even though this hadn't been his intention).

In the end Galileo was convicted of the lesser charge of "vehement suspicion of heresy," the court banned the *Dialogue*, and Galileo was forced to formally recant his views. Documents detailing his conviction were widely circulated, largely at the behest of Pope Urban VIII, who was keen to make an example of him. Within these documents (as explained by Maurice A. Finocchiaro in *Galileo Goes to Jail and Other Myths About Science and Religion*), it was said that Galileo was subjected to "rigorous examination" during the interrogation process and that he was to be imprisoned for an indefinite period within the Inquisition jails in Rome. While torture was never mentioned, most assumed that "rigorous examination" implied torture and that Galileo was indeed imprisoned in what many envisaged to be a miserable and dark cell.

However, documents that were unearthed in the eighteenth and nineteenth centuries show that Galileo's "imprisonment"—with the possible exception of three days in June 1633—consisted of lodging under house arrest in a number of rather grand houses around Italy, including the Tuscan Embassy and, for a five-month period, the home of his good friend the Archbishop of Siena. Thereafter he resided at his own villa on house arrest, just outside Florence, until his death in 1642. During these times of "arrest," he spent his time working on one of his finest works, the *Discourses on Two New Sciences*.

The subsequent publication of documents relating to the trial (including minutes of an Inquisition meeting) in the late nineteenth century also reveal that it was highly unlikely that Galileo was tortured.

REALITY CHECK

GALILEO'S *DIALOGUE*

Released in 1632, Galileo's *Dialogue on the Two Great World Systems* debated the two conflicting theories on the order of the universe: the geocentric or Aristotelian view that the Earth is the center of the universe (the basis of most European thought at that time) and the heliocentric or Copernican view that the Sun is the center of the universe. In Galileo's *Dialogue*, the Copernican view, which appeared to contradict the Holy Scriptures (although Galileo was adamant that it didn't) and the "orthodox" scientific opinion of the day, ultimately won the debate. While its publication caused considerable controversy within the Italian states, Galileo considered himself a good Catholic and believed that science and religion could be reconciled. In fact, prior to the *Dialogue* he had befriended several cardinals, including the man who became Pope Urban VIII, and had dedicated his 1613 publication *Letters on Sunspots* to Pope Paul III. Indeed, prior to 1632 the Church largely accepted his science; it was the universities, steeped in the cosmology of Aristotle, who opposed him.

MINI MYTH

THE TELESCOPE

Galileo is generally credited as the inventor of the telescope. In fact, someone else came up with the idea, although sources vary on who this may have been. A popular candidate is the Dutch eyeglass-maker Hans Lippershey who in 1608 created a device consisting of two glasses in a tube that magnified distant objects. Others believe that, even earlier, Leonard Digges (c. 1520–c. 1559), an English mathematician and father of the astronomer Thomas Digges, invented the first reflecting and refracting telescopes, although political circumstances prevented him capitalizing on his invention. Galileo substantially improved Lippershey's model (even though he hadn't actually seen it) and made a telescope with three times the magnification (and later thirty times the magnification). Using this more powerful telescope, Galileo was able to develop his revolutionary theories on astronomy to include the examination of Jupiter and its orbiting four satellites (moons), which, he deduced, disproved the accepted geocentric view of cosmology.

It was rare for Inquisitors to torture defendants in Rome, and rules forbade the torture of the elderly or the sick. (Galileo was sixty-nine and suffering from arthritis and a hernia.) Strict Inquisition rules also decreed that any torture had to be put to formal vote, of which there is again no reference. The worst that may have happened to Galileo is that he was *threatened* with torture; had he been physically tortured (which generally involved tying the victim's hands behind his back and suspending them from the ceiling, often resulting in dislocation of the shoulders), it's highly unlikely he would have been well enough to have attended the rest of the trial.

Bloody Mary was a ruthless persecutor of English Protestants.

Queen Mary I or "Bloody Mary," as she is commonly known, is remembered as a religious persecutor — a childless Tudor queen who mercilessly burnt at the stake hundreds, if not thousands, of Protestants in her quest to restore Catholicism in England. Mary did execute 290 religious dissenters and Protestants, and while this was not an insignificant number, neither was it extraordinarily high compared to the brutality of the times. Mary's sister, Elizabeth I, burnt just as many Catholics, and their father Henry VIII killed off thousands more during his reign.

Mary I has remained, in the words of the historian Linda Porter, one of the "most maligned and misunderstood of all monarchs." Frequently depicted as a weak-willed Catholic bigot, her reign has always compared unfavorably with the "golden age" of Elizabeth I. As the first Queen of England, Mary was assumed to be imbued with the "feminine" traits of fierce emotion and unbridled lust. Elizabeth, however, showed more masculine traits, proclaiming that though she had the "body of a weak and feeble woman" she had the "heart and stomach of a king."

Mary's Spanish heritage (her mother was Catherine of Aragon) and marriage to the Spanish king, Philip II, further entrenched her in the world of Catholicism and provoked deep suspicion among the English populace. Her desperate and failed attempts to produce a child proved her greatest tragedy undermining her marriage and ultimately leading to Protestant succession.

And yet when Mary was crowned in 1553, there was jubilation among the populace as ballads, sermons, and poems celebrated the ascension of a warrior queen and deliverer. In securing the throne, Mary had shown considerable determination and fortitude (far removed from her supposedly weak-willed nature), mustering men and support, causing the Privy Council to switch its allegiance from the incumbent Lady Jane Grey to Mary. Again, in 1554, Mary as Queen rallied Londoners with a rousing speech and shut down Thomas Wyatt and his army of rebels who were opposed to her intended marriage to Philip II. In an attempt to pacify the country and to dampen rumors that she was selling England to Spain, Mary proclaimed that she was married to the realm first.

In July 1554, the royal marriage went ahead, whereupon Mary, who had initially shown some moderation toward her religious adversaries, pressed ahead with her plans to restore papal jurisdiction in England. In the autumn of that year, the heresy laws of the fifteenth century (which allowed for burning as a penalty) were revived, and all of Henry VIII's statutes against papal authority were repealed. Around eight hundred Protestants—including the English historian John Foxe (see page 140)—fled the country, while those who continued to defend their Protestant faith were subject to persecution under the heresy laws.

The executions began with four clergymen in February 1555 and continued with the burning of Bishops Hugh Latimer and Nicholas Ridley, as well as the Archbishop of Canterbury, Thomas Cranmer, who, despite having recanted and repudiated Protestant theology, was condemned to death. With Cardinal Reginald Pole as Archbishop of Canterbury, the burnings continued, largely in the eastern regions of England, where Protestantism was more entrenched.

The common perception is that these executions, also known as the Marian Persecutions, turned its victims into martyrs of the Protestant cause, thus influencing public opinion against Catholicism and Mary's government. Eamon Duffy in his book *Fires of Faith* argues, however, that the burnings were largely accepted by the general populace. The real cause for growing discontent with Mary was her Spanish marriage, her pro-Spanish policies, and war with France, which led to French forces seizing Calais, England's remaining foothold in mainland Europe, in January 1558. Combined with this, the years of Mary's reign were also persistently wet, which resulted in failed harvests and famine.

MINI MYTH

THE ORIGINS OF THE BLOODY MARY MYTH

The maligning of Mary's image began as soon as her half-sister Elizabeth I took the throne in 1558, but it really gained momentum in the seventeenth century, when Protestants, who nicknamed her "Bloody Mary," used her example to highlight the dangers of Catholic rule in England. The perception of Mary as a brutal tyrant was largely shaped by two publications written by the Protestant exiles John Knox and John Foxe. Knox's *The First Blast of the Trumpet Against the Monstrous Regiment of Women*, published in 1558, attacked Mary and referred to her as a "monstrous Amazona." And John Foxe's *The Book of Martyrs*, published in 1563, "recorded in loving and gruesome detail" the lives and deaths of Mary's victims. The book went on to be a bestseller and was read almost as widely as the Bible. As Roger Lockyer in *Tudor and Stuart Britain 1471–1714* states, "Mary had given the English Protestant church its martyrs; Foxe made sure that their deeds would be an inspiration to generations of those who came after."

The reign of Mary I is now inextricably linked with the persecution of Protestants, yet in the 1550s, thousands of Protestants in the Netherlands lost their lives and far more Huguenot Protestants were burned in France (culminating in the infamous St. Bartholomew's Day Massacre of 1572 when between 5,000 and 10,000 were killed). The obsession with the Marian Persecutions also tends to overlook Mary's achievements as monarch. She improved the financial administration of government (which had been sliding toward bankruptcy during the later years of King Henry VIII's reign). She reformed the coinage; managed Parliament; and ultimately secured the throne as the first crowned Queen of England and Ireland (thereby defending the line of Tudor succession).

Mary's greatest misfortune was to die young (from fever at the age of forty-two) and childless—had she lived longer and succeeded in reestablishing Catholicism in Britain, she no doubt would have been celebrated as a valiant defender of the nation's faith. Instead, her history was written by Protestants, who bequeathed to us the image of Mary as a ruthless persecutor of Protestants, an image that, however distorted, is still as prevalent today as it was in the days of John Foxe.

St. Patrick was Irish.

On St. Patrick's Day (March 17), millions of people around the world dress in green, don a shamrock, and celebrate all things Irish. As the patron saint of Ireland, the fifth-century apostle St. Patrick is seen as the very embodiment of Ireland and a true Irishman in every sense. However, he was in fact born in Britain; his original name was Maewyn Succat; and he didn't go to Ireland until the age of sixteen.

Two letters written in Latin, which are generally accepted to have been written by St. Patrick, provide the details we have on the apostle's life. He was born in (or around) 387 CE to a Romanized British family in, as he tells us in his *Confessio*, the settlement of "Bannavem Taburniae." This place name now does not exist on any current map of Britain, although locations suggested include Kilpatrick in Scotland, Banwen in Wales, and somewhere between Chester and the Solway Firth.

Patrick tells us that when he was sixteen he was captured by a gang of Irish pirates and taken as a slave to Ireland. There he spent six years herding sheep and tending pigs, again at an uncertain location possibly in County Mayo or at Slemish Mountain in County Antrim. It was during these years that he turned with fervor to his faith and spent much of his time praying.

Patrick finally managed to escape captivity in Ireland by stowing away on a boat bound for Britain, and he eventually returned to live with his parents. Having been trained and ordained a priest, he returned to Ireland in 432 CE, inspired, as he wrote in *Confessio*, by a dream in which a voice that said to him (as translated from the Latin), "We beg you, holy youth, that you shall come and shall walk again among us."

He answered his calling and returned to Ireland as the country's second bishop. Now known as Patrick, he went on to baptize and convert thousands of people and bring the message of Christianity to much of Ireland. However, Patrick was not Ireland's first Christian missionary, as there were already other Christian believers in the country. Ireland had strong trading links with the Roman Empire and therefore would have been touched by Christianity in some way. In the fifth century, Pope Celestine I is said to have sent Ireland its first bishop, Palladius, and he may well have joined other clerics already administering to existing Christian communities in Ireland.

Following a fairly turbulent life as a bishop in Ireland (during which time he was robbed, arrested, and accused of financial impropriety), Patrick died (it is said) on March 17, 461 CE (although 493 CE has also been suggested). Thereon he was largely forgotten, although during the twelfth century mythology slowly grew around the legend of Patrick. Centuries later, as part of the widespread veneration of saints and missionaries—particularly Irish ones—who continued to spread Christianity and monastic and scholarly

MINI MYTH

St. Patrick and the Snakes

Another popular myth associated with St. Patrick is that he freed Ireland from snakes by driving them into the sea after they began attacking him during a forty-day fast. According to the *Concise Oxford Dictionary of the Christian Church*, "he stood on a hill . . . and used a staff to herd the slithering creatures into the sea, banishing them for eternity." The problem with this myth is that snakes have never existed in Ireland, and still don't today. Following the last Ice Age 10,000 years ago, snakes returned to northern and western Europe, but never returned to Ireland as it was protected by the surrounding seas. (In fact, Ireland, along with Greenland, Iceland, New Zealand, and Antarctica, are the few places in the world which are completely snake free zones.) The story has a more metaphorical meaning: snakes often symbolize evil and the driving out of the snakes more likely refers to Patrick's mission to rid Ireland of its evil, pagan influence.

traditions when the rest of Europe had fallen to warring tribes, Patrick was honored as the patron saint of Ireland.

Saint Patrick's feast day has been observed in Ireland as a fairly minor religious holiday for centuries. In the main, it's Irish immigrants living abroad, particularly those living in the United States, who, in a bid to reconnect with their Irish roots, have turned St. Patrick's Day into a much bigger celebration. The first St. Patrick's Day parades were held by Irish soldiers fighting in the Revolutionary War, and hundreds of parades and celebrations are now held in the United States, Canada, Australia, and across the world. In Ireland, St. Patrick's Day has also become more commercialized (up until the 1970s all pubs in Ireland were closed on St. Patrick Day), and hundreds of thousands of people now take part in Dublin's multi-day celebrations.

So the truth is out: St. Patrick was not Irish, nor did he alone establish Christianity in Ireland. But perhaps the old adage that "everybody's Irish on St. Patrick's Day" applies just as much to St. Patrick as it does to those celebrating his memory.

Roman gladiators fought to the death.

I t's a popular belief that the citizens of Ancient Rome liked to spend much of their year perched high up in the amphitheater, where they could revel in the bloodbath of the gladiatorial contests below. Gladiators fighting to the death or slaying an array of exotic animals provided a captivating spectacle. It also created an image of Roman brutality that still holds great fascination today in movies, books, and television shows on premium channels featuring scantily clad actors whose togas surely would not have been considered practical attire in ancient times. Yet the reality of gladiatorial contests was quite different from this common perception. Combat developed during the Roman period as part of a funeral rite and eventually became a highly organized public spectacle in which the death of the gladiator was no longer the ultimate goal.

Indeed, much of what we know (or think we know) about gladiatorial combat is mired in misconception that was shaped in relatively recent years by the Hollywood blockbusters *Spartacus* (1960) and *Gladiator* (2000). It's an area of history often subject to vivid imaginings and supposition as little survives from the period to tell us exactly what happened during gladiatorial games. Contemporary accounts, written histories, Roman mosaics, and other pictorial images give some background clues, but written descriptions of actual gladiatorial matches are few and far between (see box on facing page).

REALITY CHECK
LIBER SPECTACULORUM

The only surviving detailed account of a gladiatorial battle comes from the Roman poet Martial. The poem, from his *Liber Spectaculorum*, describes a battle between the gladiators Verus and Priscus held in 80 CE, on the first day of Emperor Titus's games at the Colosseum in Rome. It's an evenly matched fight ("equal they fought, equal they yielded"). Both are declared victors, and both are granted the *rudis*, or wooden sword, by Titus, which signified their freedom.

The gladiatorial games, during which armed combatants ("gladiators," meaning "swordsmen") fought against each other, evolved from an Etruscan funeral rite in which the dead were honored with offerings of blood. These *munera*, as they were called, were believed to have been introduced to Rome in 216 BCE, when the sons of Marcus Lepidus honored their deceased father by setting three pairs of gladiators against each other in a fight to the death. In 46 BCE, Julius Caesar, having commemorated his father in a similar way, hosted a munera at the tomb of his daughter Julia, who had died in childhood eight years previously. An elaborate affair, large numbers were killed — including several of Caesar's own soldiers.

Gradually the munera became separated from the funerary context and evolved into a very public display of wealth and prestige by the aristocratic elite. In Rome the emperors eventually assumed control of the "gladiatorial games," and by the time of Trajan (98 CE to 117 CE), military victories were celebrated by as many as 5,000 pairs of gladiators. By the end of the second century CE, writer Tertullian in *De spectaculis* (part XII) complained that "this class of public entertainment has passed from being a compliment to the dead to being a compliment to the living."

For these more public spectacles, gladiators were no longer required to fight to the death (unlike the more private munera, for which death was a necessary outcome). The running order of events at these gladiatorial games often followed a standard formula: animal fights or hunts in the morning (usually fought not by gladiators as such but by condemned criminals known as *bestiarii* or by trained animal hunters known as *venatores*), then a variety of special features, which could include the execution of criminals and "comedy fights," followed by the gladiatorial contests in the afternoon.

The main sponsor of the games was known as the "editor," and many matches employed a senior referee and an assistant (as depicted in many mosaics featuring gladiatorial combat). These referees would keep a close eye on the proceedings, while deferring to the judgment of the editor, who would decide the fate of a defeated combatant (based largely on the mood of the crowd). While the exact details surrounding the rules of combats are lost, the existence of these mediators suggests the matches were well organized and subject to complex regulations.

It's thought that the combatants, rather than fighting each other in a great free-for-all, more commonly fought in evenly matched pairs, with one style of gladiator (there were seven categories of fighters) pitted against another style. A *retarius* gladiator, for example, who was lightly armed with a net and trident, might be paired with the more heavily armed, but less mobile, *secutor*. These gladiators—who were mostly slaves, prisoners of war, and the occasional free-born volunteer—received rigorous training, lots of food and medical attention, and were thus viewed by their trainers (*lanistae*) as valuable commodities, not to be dispatched lightly. The top gladiators might fight only two or three times a year, and some gladiators survived to reach retirement. If a gladiator died during combat, a *lanista* might well expect the game's editor to pay heavy compensation, thus making any

MINI MYTH
THUMBS UP / THUMBS DOWN

It's popularly thought that Roman spectators would decide the fate of a defeated gladiator by showing either a "thumbs down" for death, or "thumbs up" if they thought he should be spared. However, one of the only direct references to this hand gesture comes from the Roman poet Juvenal, who wrote in his *Satire III* that the Roman mob indicated who should be slain by "a turn of the thumb." The problem is we don't know which way the thumb was turned: some historians claim it was turned upward, others downward or in a sideways motion. And there is little evidence to corroborate Juvenal's reference (Martial wrote that a crowd appealed for mercy by waving a handkerchief or by shouting). If a gladiator wished to surrender, it's thought that he would lay down his arms and raise his index finger, usually his left one, as a gesture of asking for mercy to the crowd. The referee would then stop the match and would refer to the editor or emperor if a final decision needed to be made.

gladiatorial bloodbath an expensive outcome for the game organizers.

It's been estimated that during the first century CE, there was a ninety percent survival rate among gladiators. In a society where life and death hung in precarious balance, where half of Rome's population would die before their twentieth birthday, the professional gladiator, fighting for the entertainment of the masses, would fare much better than many of his spectators. So, while death was a certainty for any condemned criminals who entered the arena, few bouts—probably a maximum of one in ten—ended in the death of a gladiator.

The idea that Roman gladiators fought to the death has been propounded throughout history, and has been more recently popularized with the release of gladiator-themed Hollywood blockbusters. Yet, while historical evidence of actual combat is scarce, what does survive challenges the common perception that gladiators fought to the death.

Vichy France leader Philippe Pétain tried to save Jews from the Holocaust.

Set up after the German invasion of France, the Vichy Government of 1940 to 1945 was headed by World War I veteran Philippe Pétain. As a collaborative government, Pétain's administration maintained legal authority over roughly two-fifths of France, with the capital situated in the central spa town of Vichy. By 1939 France had the second largest population of Jews in Europe (some 330,000), half of whom were European refugees who had fled to France in the hope that they would be protected from persecution. However, between 1942 and 1945 the Vichy regime transported nearly 76,000 Jewish refugees and French citizens to Nazi concentration camps. Pétain always claimed he opposed their deportation and that he had in fact tried everything he could to stop it, but increasing evidence has come to light to suggest he and other Vichy officials were fully complicit in the deportation.

The image of Pétain as reluctant Nazi collaborator and innocent bystander during the Holocaust persisted in France for more than half a century, much of it borne from a general unwillingness to revisit the "dark years" of the Vichy regime. For decades, common perception had it that the Vichy government shielded the French from the worst evils of Nazi rule, an argument reinforced by Robert Aron in his major 1954 historical work *Histoire de Vichy*. The popular view was that Pétain, the great hero of World War I's Battle of Verdun, skillfully played off the Germans while in secret negotiations with the Allies, and it was his pro-Nazi Prime Minister Pierre Laval ("the Germans' man") who was largely to blame for the anti-Jewish sentiment within Vichy.

But in 1972 the publication of a book by American historian Robert Paxton, *Vichy France: Old Guard and New Order 1940–1944*, demolished this image of the Vichy regime, reigniting a bitter debate in France. Having examined both French and German records, Paxton showed that Pétain wasn't playing any sort of double game with the Nazis, that the Germans in fact gave Pétain enormous freedom of action, and that the Vichy regime's ultimate aim was to establish itself within the Nazi new order of France.

In 1981 another book by Paxton and Michael Marrus, *Vichy France and the Jews*, argued that anti-Semitism was at the very heart of the Vichy regime and that Vichy officials and police were directly involved in the rounding up of Jews to the east. Six years later, in 1987, the bringing to trial of Klaus Barbie, the German chief of the Gestapo in Lyon, further highlighted

A map of Vichy France, 1940 to 1944

the involvement of the Vichy regime in the Holocaust, as did the jailing of one of his French aides, Paul Touvier, in 1992.

It wasn't until 1995 that Jacques Chirac, who had succeeded ex-Vichy official François Mitterrand as president of France, apologized to the Jews for "the criminal insanity of the occupying power [that] was assisted by [the] French State," breaking with the long-standing conviction that Vichy was an illegal aberration that did not represent France. And the 1998 imprisonment of ex-cabinet minister Maurice Papon for his involvement in the deportation of Jews from Bordeaux finally established the complicity of the French in the Holocaust. Since then, France has paid compensation and returned property to survivors, and opened up a wealth of previously undisclosed archives relating to the Vichy government.

In 2010, the anonymous donation of a previously unseen document to the Holocaust Memorial Museum in Paris provided an unsettling insight into the first anti-Jewish legislation of the Vichy regime. Enacted in October 1940, the statute excluded Jews from a wide range of professions, leading to the confiscation of Jewish property and a broad system of anti-Semitic measures that later facilitated the holding and

deportation of Jews to Nazi death camps. Throughout
1940 and 1941 more than 40,000 refugees were held
in French concentration camps, while in 1941 French
police began mass arrests of Jewish people. In August 1942 Vichy police hunted down Jewish refugees,
seized Jewish families from their homes, and transported around 11,000 men, women, and children to the
Drancy internment camp outside Paris (a main transit
center for Auschwitz). During 1942, Vichy officials
sent 41,951 Jews to Germany, then another 31,889 in
1943 and 1944. Out of 75,721 Jewish deportees, fewer
than 2,000 survived.

Part of the draft bill for the 1940 anti-Jewish legislation, the newly donated document contained numerous annotations that experts have authenticated
as Pétain's own handwriting. The document reveals
that the statute originally excluded the descendants
of Jews who were born French or naturalized before
1860. Pétain's alleged amendments crossed out the ex-
clusion clause and made the statute applicable to all
Jews, both foreign and French, and barred them from
a wider range of professions.

The historian and lawyer Serge Klarsfeld, who un-
veiled the document, said, "This document establishes
Pétain's decisive role in drawing up this position in the

most aggressive way," indicating that Laval was not solely responsible for the regime's anti-Semitic measures. It also destroys the still widely held myth that Pétain and the Vichy regime sought to protect French Jews over refugee Jews (as at least double the percentage of non-French Jews died between 1940 and 1944 as compared to 15 percent of French Jews).

Right from the outset of the Vichy regime, it's clear that Pétain never had any intention to save Jews, French or otherwise, from deportation. Moreover, as Klarsfeld says, "Pétain not only intervened to push legislation against Jews further than proposed, but created an entire anti-Semitic outlook and framework that in 1940 was even harsher than what the Germans had adopted." The unveiling of this document marks another major step in history's reexamination of Pétain, further demolishing the now dwindling argument that he strove to protect Jews living in France from the Holocaust.

Thanksgiving Day harks back to the "First Thanksgiving" given by Plymouth settlers in 1621.

Thanksgiving Day is a time for families to feast, watch football, take in a parade, and to give thanks, of course, for the many blessings of the past year. The common assumption is that the celebration owes its origins to the "first Thanksgiving" of 1621, when New England settlers in Plymouth gave thanks to God for a bountiful harvest following a particularly harsh winter (during which 46 of the 102 pilgrims had died). According to the only contemporary account we have of the event, written by the Pilgrim leader Edward Winslow in *Mourt's Relation*, the feasting and recreation took place over three days and included the participation of ninety Wampanoag Indians and their chief, Massasoit, who donated five deer to the celebrations.

The origins of Thanksgiving, however, are not quite so clear-cut and, like many commonly accepted traditions, appear to be a blurring of myth and fact. To begin with, the events of 1621 did not technically constitute the "first Thanksgiving." Celebrations to give thanks for a good harvest or any kind of good fortune is a ritual common to cultures all around the world, and they were certainly performed in America before 1621. Indeed, for millennia Native Americans have performed rituals giving thanks for all the gifts of life. Settlers in Newfoundland in 1578 probably held one of the first colonial services

You realize this means we'll have to invite them back to our place.

REALITY CHECK
A COVER-UP JOB

Neither the Wampanoag Indians nor the British settlers referred to the harvest feast of 1621 as a "Thanksgiving." Some theorists have suggested that the three-day event was more likely a series of political meetings to secure a military alliance. Neither side trusted the other fully, and the arrival of ninety American Indians (all of them men) following the sound of gunshot from the British hunters was probably an act of military precaution. For many Native Americans, Thanksgiving represents the conquest and genocide of their people, and some have accused the United States of fabricating the Thanksgiving story in a bid to whitewash the injustice caused to the indigenous peoples of America.

of Thanksgiving (a combination of age-old traditions of harvest festivals and religious services), as had the Spanish settlers in Florida some years before that.

The idea of holding a Thanksgiving holiday did start to gain more popularity following the feast of 1621. In 1623, after the Plymouth settlers' prayers during a drought were followed by some much-needed rain, they held a Thanksgiving service even greater than the ceremony they'd held two years previously. Governor Bradford proclaimed it a day of Thanksgiving in the form of prayers and thanks to God. From then on, the occasional day of Thanksgiving, in the form of prayers for any kind of auspicious event, was held—albeit sporadically and at a very local level.

It wasn't until 1777 that regular Thanksgiving ceremonies took place, when the Continental Congress declared the first national day of Thanksgiving (largely in response to the defeat of the British at Saratoga during the Revolutionary War). Later in the century, various congressional representatives pushed for the adoption of a legal holiday of Thanksgiving, but questions were raised over its legitimacy and date. Presidents Washington, Adams, and Monroe issued further proclamations for a day of national Thanksgiving, although presidents Jefferson and Jackson objected to the national government's involvement in a religious observance. By the 1850s most states celebrated Thanksgiving but often on different dates.

President Abraham Lincoln, in the middle of the Civil War, was the first to declare Thanksgiving a national holiday in the hope that it might unite a war-torn country. The date Lincoln chose was August 6, although it was moved arbitrarily to the last Thursday of November the following year. (And here it has roughly remained, bar a two-year interlude during the Depression when Franklin D. Roosevelt brought it forward by a week in a bid to lengthen the Christmas shopping season.)

It wasn't until the mid-nineteenth century that Thanksgiving became particularly associated with the harvest celebration of 1621. The establishment of the national holiday of Thanksgiving came just after a renewed interest in the Pilgrims and the Wampanoag, caused partly by the recovery of the lost manuscript *Of Plimoth Plantation* by Governor Bradford (a retrospective journal describing the early days of the Plymouth colony) in 1855, along with Henry Wadsworth Longfellow's poem *The Courtship of Miles Standish* in 1858. The idea was also imbedded by the antiquarian Alexander Young, who commented in 1841 when he published the pilgrim leader Edward Winslow's previously lost account of the harvest meal of 1621, "This was the first Thanksgiving, the harvest festival of New England."

By the beginning of the twentieth century, the harvest meal of 1621 had begun to be taught to school children as a lesson on being good citizens. (It is still lovingly recreated and sung about in school plays and pageants across the nation.) At the same time, the holiday moved away from its religious roots, enabling immigrants in the United States to share in its tradition, while the more secular traditions of parades and sporting events grew in number.

MINI MYTH

TURKEY DINNER

The modern-day Thanksgiving meal of turkey, sweet potato pie, corn bread, mashed potatoes, cranberry sauce, and pumpkin pie is said to resemble the harvest meal of 1621. However, turkey was not specifically mentioned in Edward Winslow's account, who wrote, ". . . Our governor sent four men on fowling. . . . They four in one day killed as much fowl as, with a little help beside, served the company almost a week." While the settlers and Wampanoag ate wild turkey, at that time of year (the harvest meal was held at some point between the beginning of October and beginning of November), it's likely they hunted waterfowl, such as ducks or geese. The 1621 feast also included venison—as Winslow mentions the Wampanoag donating five deer—and it's doubtful the settlers would have had the sugar they needed to make cranberry sauce or pumpkin pie (although they may well have had pumpkins).

Thanksgiving Day still has a deep association with the events of 1621 and has come to symbolize intercultural peace and the sanctity of home, family, and the community. But it wasn't until the late nineteenth century that this association really took root. The combination of Lincoln's declaration of Thanksgiving as a national holiday and the rediscovery of lost manuscripts relating to the Plymouth settlers consolidated the idea that Thanksgiving harked back to the harvest meal of 1621, though celebrations of thanks have existed for as long ago as there were things to be thankful for.

Oliver Cromwell:
Man of the people and
common-man's hero.

In 1653, Oliver Cromwell (1599–1658) rose from provincial obscurity to become Lord Protector of England, Scotland, and Ireland, and ruler of the nation's republican Commonwealth. A revolutionary figure who rallied for the abolition of monarchy, Cromwell has gained the reputation of a common-man's hero, a man who, in opposition to aristocratic and monarchial oppression, rose from nowhere to become the most powerful man in England. And yet Cromwell hailed from aristocratic stock, and his ancestry was anything but common.

In 1599, Cromwell was born into a considerably wealthy family in Huntingdonshire, England. Several members of his family had served as JPs (Justices of the Peace) or MPs (Members of Parliament) for the county. While Cromwell's family had no hereditary

Blacker is the new black.

title — and his position as the eldest son of the younger son of a knight was considered to be socially ambiguous — various other male members of his family had also been knighted, and the family could even trace its lineage back to the great Tudor dynasty, of which Cromwell was a direct descendant. Cromwell's great-grandfather was a Welshman named Morgan ap Williams, who married Catherine Cromwell, the elder sister of Thomas Cromwell (Henry VIII's chief minister). Rather than keeping the Welsh name of Williams — which, strictly speaking, should have been Oliver Cromwell's surname — the family chose to keep the name of Cromwell, in honor of their distinguished relative. Morgan ap Williams was the grandson (by illegitimate birth) of Jasper Tudor, who was uncle to the Tudor monarch Henry VII and the son of Owen Tudor, the founder of the Tudor dynasty and husband to Catherine of Valois, the daughter of Charles VI of France. Therefore Oliver Cromwell's illustrious ancestry may have included not just the House of Tudor, but also some of the great dynasties of Europe.

Cromwell's own father, the JP Robert Cromwell, had served as a Member of Parliament under Elizabeth I. When he died in 1617, Oliver was forced to take charge of the family at the age of eighteen, looking after his widowed mother, seven unmarried sisters, and, from 1620, his own wife and growing family. It was at this point that Cromwell's social standing dipped slightly. His annual income of £100 ($155) was just enough for him to retain his gentleman status, although by 1631 he was forced to move to St. Ives, East Anglia, where he lived as a tenant farmer, dressing in plain russet like the other yeomen. But this sharp decline in his social and financial standing was relatively short-lived, as by 1636 he had inherited the control of various properties from his maternal uncle, Sir Thomas Steward, which increased his income to

£300 ($367) a year and restored him once again to the standing of a gentleman.

Despite his momentary dip in fortune, Cromwell remained exceptionally well connected, which played a vital part in his later political and military career. Between 1628 and 1629, he served as MP for Huntingdon (although he only gave one, badly received speech) alongside eight of his cousins in Parliament. His marriage to Elizabeth Bourchier, daughter of the London merchant and landowner Sir James Bourchier, also brought Cromwell into contact with a number of leading Puritan families, as well as the London merchant community and the Earls of Warwick and Holland.

In around 1628, Cromwell suffered illness and depression, which led to a profound spiritual awakening that left him with strong and uncompromising Puritan beliefs. In 1640 Cromwell returned as MP for Cambridge (a position he likely secured through his influential contacts, for he was almost certainly the least well-off man there). He is said to have arrived in Parliament shabbily dressed in a poorly tailored "plain cloth suit," his neckband splattered in blood. He was known for his passionate manner in Parliament, dropping "tears down with his words," seeming to lack the finesse and polish of some of his colleagues. Though

Cromwell may have looked to some like a country bumpkin, much of that was borne from his religious convictions, which advocated plain dress and less emphasis on outward appearance.

Cromwell's successful military career (1643–51) during the English Civil War—in which, with no previous experience as a military captain, he was promoted first to colonel and then to senior officer—radically improved his financial circumstances. As early as 1641–42, he was able to pledge quite large sums (between £1,200 to £2,000—$1,850 and $3,100) toward reconquering Ireland. His military salary combined with the granting of extensive lands across England led to a considerable fortune of well in excess of £10,000 ($15,500) per year. As Lord Protector (1653–58), his standing as the most powerful man in England brought him even greater personal wealth.

Cromwell's rise, particularly in the context of the seventeenth century, was indeed meteoric, and his style of government revolutionary in that there were hints of something approaching democracy. While for a short time his position dipped below that of a gentleman and his religious convictions insisted on a more basic style of dress, his family lineage's strong links to the gentry and aristocracy made Cromwell far

REALITY CHECK
CROMWELL AS LORD PROTECTOR

The nature of Cromwell's role as head of the Commonwealth was revolutionary, but his aim was never to reform the social order or to extend the rights of the common man. After the turmoil of the English Civil War, his ambition as Lord Protector was to restore a stable government and to promote freedom of worship and godliness through spiritual and moral reform. Cromwell had nothing against hierarchy in state or society, proclaiming, "a nobleman, a gentleman, a yeoman, the distinction of these: that is a good interest of the nation, and a great one!" He considered the beliefs of the Levellers—a political group that called for extending the suffrage and equality before law— tantamount to anarchy. In essence, his views were those of a country gentleman, in keeping with the beliefs of his parliamentary colleagues and kinsmen.

from the common-man's hero of historical myth. Not only was he related to a distinguished Tudor statesman, but as a descendant through the male line of Owen, he was also a member of the great Tudor dynasty itself.

The U.S. Army defeated the Japanese and liberated Vietnam in 1945.

Although Vietnam was part of French Indochina in 1945, it had been occupied by Japan throughout World War II. In March of that year, Japan ousted the Vichy French and installed Emperor Bao Dai at the helm of the newly entitled Empire of Vietnam. But Japan's rule was brief and unstable, and her surrender quickly followed in September. Yet rather than the United States leading the defeat, it was actually the Vietnamese who led the resistance movement and forced the Japanese to surrender, after which the United States and its allies thwarted Vietnam's desire for independence by handing control of the country back to the French.

Disaster for France in the early stages of World War II had significant repercussions for the country's hold over its colonies. And Vietnam, geographically

remote from the West and governed by the French
since the late nineteenth century (see page 179), became an easy target for Japan, which sought to take
advantage of French weakness and extend its sphere
of influence in Southeast Asia. During World War
II, the United States—which, up until the last four
months of fighting, was still under the guidance of
the ostensibly anti-colonial Roosevelt—and its allies were complicit in Japan's endeavors. They were
skeptical of French control over Vietnam, as the
Vietnamese had been fighting the colonial rule for
decades, and encouraged France to accept Japan's
usurpation. As Bernard B. Fall outlines in *Street Without Joy*, France's decision to sign the non-aggression
pact with Thailand (Japan's ally) in 1940 indicated
collaboration on France's behalf. And thus Japan's
decisive attack on March 9, 1945, to capture any remaining French troops in Vietnam went uncontested
by the Allies.

Yet both France and Vietnam made immediate moves
to contest Japan's takeover. General de Gaulle's declaration on March 24, 1945, stated France's intention
to establish an independent regime in Vietnam and the
rest of Indochina (see page 179) while maintaining its
own sovereignty went largely unheeded. Meanwhile

charismatic Communist leader Ho Chi Minh and his national independence front, the Viet Minh, emerged as a strong nationalist presence which sought to gain independence for Vietnam. The Viet Minh had formed in 1941 and had steadily built up support by planting communist members throughout the country to recruit followers. And, as Bernard B. Fall notes, their communist training "gave them an unbeatable head start over the small idealistic nationalist groups which began to squabble over details while the Communists were taking over the country under their noses."

During the August Revolution of 1945, Ho Chi Minh and the Viet Minh forced the Japanese to surrender, and they seized power in Hanoi. On September 2, Ho Chi Minh issued the Proclamation of Independence of the Democratic Republic of Vietnam and convinced Japanese Emperor Bao Dai to resign. As Pierre Brocheux and Daniel Hémery state in *Indochina: An Ambiguous Colonization: 1858–1954*, following Japanese surrender, Indochina found itself "in a state of moral and political secession from France," and Ho Chi Minh and the Viet Minh were the best equipped to take power.

However, the world failed to cooperate, and Ho Chi Minh's government went unrecognized, despite repeated petitions to President Harry Truman asking for his support. And despite their strength in numbers, the Viet Minh were ultimately hampered by their lack of resources, which left them unable to take full advantage of the situation. They had no military, financial, or governmental power, and failed to establish effective military control following Japan's surrender.

And while Roosevelt had been hostile to French colonization, his death and Harry Truman's accession in April 1945 put a decisive end to such a stance. At the Potsdam Conference in July 1945, the Allies accepted the reestablishment of French colonial rule in Indochina; the British were entrusted with the disarmament of Japanese troops south of the 16th Parallel and the rearmament of French troops in the colonies. The spirit of colonialism was reawakened—at least in the eyes of the Allies—as France was once again seen as the rightful administrator of Indochina. Brocheux and Hémery believe that America's increasing support of France's recolonization of Indochina was a result of the threat the Soviet Union posed and the importance of France in an international context. On October 5, 1945, a telegram from the Secretary of State Dean Acheson confirmed U.S. approval of the return of Indochina to the French, and the head of the OSS

(Office of Strategic Services—precursor to the Central Intelligence Agency) William Donovan reiterated this stance when he stated it was necessary for Europe to maintain its empire in the face of Communism. France began its reconquest.

Vietnam's dreams of independence had been thwarted. The British finally left in March 1946 and handed control over to the French. But the Vietnamese nationalist spirit remained strong, and on December 19, 1946, the Viet Minh initiated the First Indochina War against the French. The war in Vietnam, which would last until 1954, had begun. And it wasn't until the end of this war, following the French defeat at Dien Bien Phu, that France's colonial grip on Vietnam was finally dissolved. However, years of fighting divided the country, with Ho Chi Minh's Communist Democratic Republic of Vietnam situated in the north, and Ngo Dinh Diem's State of Vietnam in the south. Ho Chi Minh's instigation of a guerrilla campaign against the south in the late 1950s sparked the Vietnam War, and it wasn't until July 1976 that the north and south of the country were finally united to form the Socialist Republic of Vietnam, following years of horrific bloodshed.

When the Japanese had invaded Vietnam, France's

colonial grip had been very much on the wane and Vietnam's desire for independence was growing exponentially. Ho Chi Minh and the Viet Minh were responsible for defeating the Japanese in 1945. But the decision of the United States and Allies to intervene and reinstate French colonial control only served to prolong the efforts of the Vietnamese to attain independence. Real and long-lasting independence wasn't achieved until well into the 1970s, after the North Vietnamese victory over South Vietnam. By the time of his death in 1969, Ho Chi Minh had not only defeated the Japanese, but also the French, the South Vietnamese, and the Americans, too.

REALITY CHECK
A BRIEF HISTORY OF
FRENCH INDOCHINA

France established its colonial conquest of Indochina in 1887 when a federation of the three Vietnamese regions Tonkin (north), Annam (central), and Cochinchina (south) and Cambodia was formed. Laos was added in 1893, and Kouang-Tchéou-Wan (a region on the south coast of China) in 1900. As Brocheux and Hémery state, World War II sounded the death knell of the old European empires, and France could only watch as first the Japanese and then the Vietnamese sought to take control. In 1949, Cambodia and Laos were both granted autonomy under the French Union, and their monarchies remained. But Vietnam, which was the most politically dynamic country in all of Indochina and with the best resources, came under sustained external attack. France's colonial grip on Indochina was finally halted with the proclamation of the Geneva Agreements in April 1954, which supported the territorial integrity of Indochina and declared the cessation of hostilities and foreign involvement in the region.

BIBLIOGRAPHY

⟨◦⟩

Atkins, Sinclair. *England and Wales under the Tudors*. London: Hodder Arnold, 1975.

Barham, Andrea. *Queen Elizabeth's Wooden Teeth and other Historical Fallacies*. London: Michael O'Mara Books Limited, 2007.

Boller, Paul F., Jr. *Not So! Popular Myths About America from Columbus to Clinton*. New York: Oxford University Press, 1995.

Brocheux, Pierre, and Daniel Hémery. *Indochina: An Ambiguous Colonization 1858–1954*. Berkeley, C.A.: University of California Press, 2009.

Bryson, Bill. *At Home: A Short History of Private Life*. London: Doubleday, 2010.

Bryson, Bill. *Made in America*. London: Minerva, 1998.

Corrigan, Gordon. *Mud, Blood and Poppycock*. London: Cassell, 2003.

Davies, Stevie. *A Century of Troubles England 1600–1700*. London: Channel 4, 2001.

Dikötter, Frank. *Mao's Great Famine: The History of China's Most Devastating Catastrophe 1958–62*. New York: Walker Publishing, 2010.

Donald, Graeme. *Lies, Damned Lies and History*. Charleston, S.C.: The History Press, 2010.

Fall, Bernard B. *Street Without Joy*. Mechanicsburg, P.A.: Stackpole Books, 2005.

Huntford, Roland. *Race for the South Pole — The Expedition Diaries of Scott and Amundsen*. London: Continuum, 2010.

Isaacs, Alan, ed., et al. *Oxford Dictionary of World History*. New York: Oxford University Press, 2001.

Knightley, Phillip. *Australia: A Biography of a Nation*. London: Vintage, 2001.

Lockyer, Roger. *Tudor and Stuart Britain 1471–1714*. New York: Longman Group, 1986.

The New Penguin Dictionary of Modern History 1789–1945. New York: Penguin, 2001.

Numbers, Ronald L., ed. *Galileo Goes to Jail and Other Myths About Science and Religion*. Cambridge, M.A.: Harvard University Press, 2009.

Rayner, Ed, and Ron Stapley. *Debunking History: 152 Popular Myths Exploded*. Charleston, S.C.: The History Press, 2006.

Rayner, Ed, and Ron Stapley. *Who Was Mr. Nobody? Debunking Historical Mysteries*. Gloucestershire, UK: Sutton Publishing, 2007.

Reynolds, David. *America: Empire of Liberty*. London: Penguin, 2010.

Russell, Miles, and Stuart Laycock. *UnRoman Britain: Exposing the Great Myth of Britannia*. Charleston, S.C.: The History Press, 2011.

Service, Robert. *Lenin: A Biography*. New York: Macmillan, 2000.

Snyder, Timothy. *Blood Lands: Europe Between Hitler and Stalin*. London: Basic Books, 2012.

Stone, Lawrence. *The Family, Sex and Marriage in England 1500–1800*. London: Penguin, 2000.

Weir, William. *History's Greatest Lies*. Beverly, M.A.: Fair Winds, 2009.

"Roman Britain to Anglo-Saxon England." *History Today*. 30 September 1990. historytoday.com/Catherine-hills/roman-britain-anglo-saxon-england.

Gerwarth, Robert. "Inventing the Iron Chancellor." *History Today*. June 2001.

ARTICLES AND WEBSITES

Note: Links my no longer be live at time of publication.

Archaeology.co.uk

Archaeology.org

Australianhistoryresearch.info

BBC *History* Magazine: historyextra.com

Bbc.co.uk/history

Forum.stirpes.net/revisionism/8495-top-10-myths-about-spanish-armada.html

France24.com

Guardian.co.uk

History Today: historytoday.com

Independent.co.uk

Literaryreview.co.uk

Mgsanchez.net/2008/08/writing-myth-monumentalism-and.html

News.nationalgeographic.com

NYtimes.com

Olivercromwell.org

"The Roman Gladiator." http://penelope.uchicago.edu/~grout/
    encyclopaedia_romana/gladiators/gladiators.html

"Thanksgiving History." Plimoth Plantation. plimoth.org/learn/
    thanksgiving-history.

Si.edu/Encyclopedia_SI/nmah/thanks

Telegraph.co.uk

Thesundaytimes.co.uk

Time.com

Wikipedia

INDEX

∽○∾

Note: Page numbers in *italic* refer to illustrations.

ALSO AVAILABLE FROM READER'S DIGEST

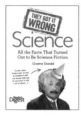

They Got It Wrong: Science

They Got It Wrong: Science gives perspective on how the way we view the workings of the world has evolved throughout history. Discover the fascinating stories behind 50 scientific theories that were once regarded as fact but history proved were pure fiction.

Graeme Donald
ISBN 978-1-62145-009-2 • $15.99 hardcover

Bible Stories You May Have Forgotten: Miracles, Adventures, and Life Lessons from Genesis to Revelation

Does the Tower of Babel ring a bell, or do you need to clean the cobwebs out of your belfry? This light and witty reference book gives readers the basics of all the stories they need to know, condensed for ease of understanding and entertainment.

James Stuart Bell and Sam O'Neal
ISBN 978-1-62145-003-0 • $14.99 hardcover

Quotable Quotes: All New Wit & Wisdom from the Greatest Minds of Our Time

The most well-known and succinct personalities of our time lend their memorable pearls of wit and wisdom—from comedians to scientists, from presidents to performers, from authors to athletes—to this updated edition of the best-selling book.

ISBN 978-1-62145-004-7 • $14.99 hardcover

The Insult Dictionary: History's Best Slights, Street Talk, and Slang

Do you long for the days when a jerk was a "cad"? Want to tell that "swillbelly" to clean up his table manners and that grumbling "glump" to stop whining? All this churlishness and more can be found in the pages of this complete(ly hilarious) guide to waxing vintage.

Julie Tibbott
ISBN 978-1-62145-066-5 • $14.99 hardcover